STO

**DO NOT REMOVE
CARDS FROM POCKET**

ALLEN COUNTY PUBLIC LIBRARY

FORT WAYNE, INDIANA 46802

You may return this book to any agency, branch,
or bookmobile of the Allen County Public Library.

Gardens for Children

Is *that* what a daisy smells like? Lawns·are ideal for crawlers

Gardens for Children

Tigger Wise

Kangaroo Press

by the same author
The Self-Made Anthropologist

Front cover: The mulberry tree is one of children's favourites (page 25)

Drawings by Sophie Wise

Photographic assistance from:
Suzanne Davies, Danny Gerber, Sophie Wise
and Grahame Wise
With special thanks to:
Maynard Davies, Lesley Rosenberg,
Jenny Sterland and Simon Wise

First published in 1986 by Kangaroo Press Pty Ltd
3 Whitehall Road (P.O. Box 75) Kenthurst 2154
Typeset by T. & H. Bayfield
Printed in Hong Kong by Colorcraft Ltd

ISBN 0-86417-066-1

Contents

All plants mentioned in this book are obtainable in Australian nurseries and all are relatively easy to grow provided some thought is given to suitability of climate and position.

Introduction

Kids love gardens. Gardens full of trees to climb and secret places to hide. Gardens with weedy corners and swinging gates and sunny lawns. To them, gardens are exciting places full of things to do and ways to have fun.

Yet many people have forgotten that kids often have surprising ideas about what makes a great garden. Unlike adults, children's favourite plants are likely to be ones we generally think of as weeds (remember blowing seeds off dandelion heads?). Unlike adults, kids' favourite places in the garden are rarely the sunny patios where we like to read our papers but some cool dark cubbyhole behind the shrubs by the back fence. And if you ask kids to name the prettiest thing in the garden, it's hardly ever the red rose or the flowering cherry, but the pansy because its flower looks like a face — or a bright scarlet autumn leaf.

If you are growing a garden where children play and you'd like to try planting some of the plants they treasure, you'll find this little book crammed with information. Use it to find the kids' climbing tree that's best (and safest) for your district. Find which home-grown vegetables children *really* like to eat. There's a chapter on gardening tricks that will have the kids mystified — and another on plants that look so amazingly like something else, their nicknames are a joke. Best of all, you'll find how easy it is to make your garden into a cheerful imaginative place children will remember forever.

Hide and seek would be fun among the dapples and tangles of this big wooded back garden

Children rarely play in a vast exposed front garden like this though the fence is a good climbing one and there is a useful tap

Big gardens are fun for older children, especially with a gravel drive to crunch under their bike wheels

Far too formal, bare and exposed for most children

1 Things Children Like (and Don't Like) about Everyday Gardens

As any child will tell you, a *proper* garden is one you can *do* things in — parents who truthfully remember their childhood would have to agree. However, this doesn't mean your garden has to enter a phase of total horticultural hibernation and homely squalour lasting throughout the child-raising years. While it is true that children have different demands of the garden from adults, it is equally true that if the adult gardener is prepared to take into account some general principles regarding children's behaviour in the garden, then both gardener and children will find themselves enjoying what they both can feel is a proper garden. After all, a garden full of active human beings is one of the most attractive things about living in Australia.

Children rarely use the front garden. They find front gardens too public, too formal and too exposed. If the adult gardener remembers this when planting, it will reduce confrontations. Orchids planted in the front garden are less likely to have their spikes knocked off by a ball.

Children don't care what a garden looks like aesthetically. They are much more interested in the fun they can have in it and the secret hidey-holes it offers.

A very large garden does not always look welcoming to very young children. Most young children feel more secure in a small enclosed garden; ideally, they need a flat fenced-off area near the house for a few years. Terrace houses and semis with their small safe back courtyards are generally excellent for very young children.

On the other hand, for 6 years and upwards, the bigger the garden the better. Older children love to have enough room to build a bonfire on cracker night, have a game of cricket, ride their bikes and play hide and seek. As they mature, the garden can incorporate more sophisticated things like barbecues, pools, hammocks.

Children like order. A well-kept garden with swept paths and trimmed lawns gives children a sense of comfort and stability. Many children find a neglected garden with dandelions pushing up a cracked concrete path very depressing and sad.

But children also like the wild parts of the garden. In the untidy parts, they feel free and uninhibited. Traditionally weeds have always belonged to children — to pick, play with and destroy without reprimand. The untidy parts are often threaded with secret passageways and routes and hidey-holes.

Children like to go round and round. Dead ends are a no-no with children — they like to run round in circles. A flower bed dug in the centre of the lawn, or a centrally placed shrub or tree gives them something to chase each other round. In a

Two much-used ingredients of a children's garden: a big lawn and a free-standing shrub to play chasings around

Rocks make wonderful 'places' to play

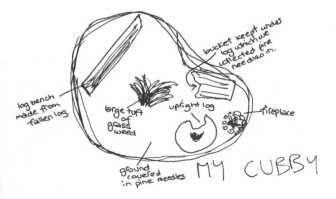

very small garden, a bird-bath or a fountain centrally placed provides a focus. Children especially like gardens that flow round all four sides of the house.

Children need territories and 'places'. What appears to an adult to be a normal back yard with its clothes lines, its rose bed, its vegetable patch and barbecue corner is in fact a collection of very different places to the child's eye. The Jungle. The Tunnel. The Whale Rock. Every rectangular suburban yard can be arranged so that there are a few 'places' for children. Under a spreading tree such as a poinciana can be a 'place'. Behind the garage another 'place'. A cubby can be made under a small bush like the weeping bottlebrush (*Callistemon viminalis*) or the yellow jasmine (*Jasminum mesneyi*). Often girls' places and boys' places are strongly differentiated. They especially like dark cool hidden 'places'.

Children like privacy. They like feeling they are far from the eyes of the house even if they are just down at the back fence. When planning a garden, consider the sight lines from the house and place garden beds, shrubs and hedges so they shield a part of the garden from full view. Good plants for this purpose include dense bushy shrubs like hydrangeas, camellias or rhododendrons.

Children like surprise. Gardens with several separate sections to them are enjoyed more than gardens you can see all at once. To see the whole garden at a glance is boring. Try planting an unexpected clump of snowdrops behind a tree. Design a path so the end can't be seen. Place a big clam shell for a bird-bath in a far corner.

Children like forbidden places. No matter how disciplined children are, they *will* get into forbidden spots like the shed roof or the junk pile. Remember, dares are a big thing in childhood. They especially like getting under things. Periodically check the garden for dangers: electrical wires, spiders, snakes, rusty up-turned nails, bottles of insecticide, two-stroke mower fuel.

The best paths twist and turn mysteriously

Children have time. Every garden needs a spot where children can sit and do nothing … a lawn, a verandah or even a broad friendly step outside the back door.

Children don't notice the view. Objects in the immediate vicinity are their concern. An apple tree outside the window is far more interesting to them than a rolling landscape. If you can build them a window box outside their bedroom window, so much the better.

If your garden is too small, build a shelf outside the bedroom window where a child can house a motley collection of plants in various stages of decrepitude

Kids *are* destructive

Children are destructive. They whip the buds off the agapanthus with a stick. They gouge holes in the sandstone rocks to make ochre. They unfurl the fern fronds. They carve their names on tree trunks. The gardener must make some firm rules about particularly precious plants — and stick to them.

On the other hand, children like indestructible plants. It is demoralising if everything in the garden breaks or crushes as a result of ordinary play. The best gardens have a few sturdy things: a bed of springy ferns to roll on, a tough hedge to bounce off, a tree that will take assorted boards nailed to its trunk.

Children like water and dirt. Making mud islands,

Catching tadpoles in the fishpond is a childhood must

11

channelling, damming, racing sticks down the drain … If you have a garden and children, you might have to put off purchasing a white carpet for the living room for a few years because playing in the mud in the backyard is one of the best things about having a garden to a child. Two things will make life easier: a garden tap installed by the back door, and an old washable rug put down as a supplementary doormat on muddy days.

Children rarely work in the garden. Giving them a plot of their own is tantamount to creating a weed patch once the initial enthusiasm has worn off. However, they do like 'helping' — by jumping in the pile of leaves that has just been raked up, or expertly spilling the packet of carrot seeds in a heap *beside* the carefully marked-out row.

Children enjoy low things. Having a line of vision a metre or so below that of adults gives a different perspective on the garden. They like little flowers that just pop out of the ground:

'Mum… I picked you a bunch of flowers'

Virginia stock, Sweet Alice, grape hyacinths, violets. They like to tip up a terracotta pot and find the slaters underneath, or to watch an ant pull a crumb along. They love jumping off low things like logs or sawn-off stumps.

Children are more interested in the nearest worm or snail than in a flock of high-flying birds…

…though Christmas beetles are fun too (if their claws don't dig into your skin)

Children like garden creatures … but different garden creatures from adults. Children prefer creatures they can get their hands on: cicadas, worms, ladybirds, lizards (because they grow new tails), Christmas beetles, stick creatures, fireflies to chase at night. They do not like bull ants, wasps and bronze citrus beetles that smell.

Children enjoy challenging things. They like a difficult tree to climb, a clump of prickly bushes to tunnel through, or a tall garden wall to walk along like a tightrope walker.

Children enjoy scary things. Scary places are part of the garden mystique. The lonely side passage with the big leaves that jerk and rattle overhead. The bulky blue-tongue lizard that flicks his eerie blue tongue. Older children often tell younger ones spooky stories about bunyips in certain parts of the garden and all children enjoy being scared of the haunted house just down the street.

A pretty garden, but too crowded for children. About the only thing a child could *do* here is swing round the verandah pole

Children like open space. Even the smallest courtyard garden should leave enough unplanted space for children to be able to run about; children don't like an all-jungle garden that leaves no room to play, or even an all-pool garden, despite their love of pools.

Children like ritual. A favourite pet's grave down the bottom of the garden, the daily feeding of the chooks or a familiar bell that calls them in to dinner are an important part of their lives. Traditional rituals like 'step on the crack and you'll break your mother's back' have been handed down for years. And as for kids' backyard clubs — they have as many ritual procedures as the local RSL, not to mention the ritual sweepings of the cubby during domestic games.

Children don't like change. If you are reworking the garden — even for their benefit — do it in small sections. Children hate to see a plant go, even a horrid prickly one. A garden should be a place where children can feel a favourite tree belongs to them

Children have extraordinary tastes in weather. Windy days send them rushing round the backyard in wild excitement. Frost has them crackling the grass underfoot with delight and shrieking at the frozen cat's milk. Hail not only has them rushing wildly to every window in the house to see where it's bouncing best, but

excavating the freezer to make way for handfuls of dirty ice and having contests with their friends to see whose keeps the longest.

Children's roots are formed in the garden. Children whose family backgrounds are in another country can keep a link with their origins through the garden. Families from Mediterranean countries could plant a grape

For families with Italian ancestry, plant a grape vine over the trellis

vine or an olive tree. Children with a Scottish background would enjoy seeing heather (*Calluna vulgaris*) grow. Children of families from the Philippines might enjoy planting a banana palm to recall their parents' or grandparents' original home.

Handicapped children have special needs. Children in wheelchairs need wide smooth pathways and flowers set in elevated beds and plenty of interesting things to look at such as fish ponds and bird-feeding bells. Blind children need plants that smell wonderful like mint, coconut geranium, jasmine, gardenia or lemon-scented gum. Perhaps a fountain that makes a gentle splashing noise would be good, or plants that make a noise such as albizzia trees with their rattly seed-pods. Plants that hurt — like rose bushes or sharp lemon grass — must be especially avoided.

13

Nostalgia

The power of the garden to evoke memories of childhood is remarkable. Ask an adult about the garden of his childhood and he can often tell you every bush, tree and blade of grass that was there.

'The smell of stock. That's what I remember most strongly. My grand-mother had this beautiful old Italian garden with a grape vine and grapes. I remember picking violets with her. I remember the wisteria just dripping down from above.'

'On Sunday afternoons, we had to drive out and visit my grandmother and grandfather. Their house had a tiny square backyard with a huge persimmon tree right in the middle. While the adults sat on the verandah and ate afternoon tea (gem scones I remember) we kids used to just run round and round the persimmon tree.'

'Right down the back were the chooks and it was my job to collect the eggs. One day, a tiger escaped from a travelling circus and couldn't be found. I had to go down and get the eggs. I was terrified I would be eaten by the tiger.'

'Aunty Blue came to live with us during the war and she made a Victory Garden. We had mustard and cress, radishes and baby squash. And tomatoes. Blue's tomatoes! We had tomatoes coming out our ears. We made pickles and tomato sauce and chutney. We gave tomatoes to the nuns up the road. We gave tomatoes to the whole of Hunter's Hill.'

'We had lots of fruit trees and mother made jam. My brother and I used to climb the old walnut tree because it gave us access to the neighbour's quince tree. We would lean over and pick the quinces when they were yellow and take one bite and bury them because they weren't nice.'

'I remember thinking we must be very rich to have such a garden. It sloped down to a sort of creek at the back with overhanging trees. Not enough to swim in, but enough to build dams and catch worms and sail boats. There were blackberries there too. You could tunnel a patch into them with the big gums overhead. We collected blackberries in kerosene tins and made pies with the pastry held up on an upside-down cup.'

'The noise in the great big fir trees was nice — big crows slept up there. We weren't allowed to play in some places because of the snakes; there were whip snakes among the white quartz stones. We used to climb up the windmill — not allowed, but we did. We built a toilet on the garage roof: four bricks covered in ivy. Frogs came out the tap into the bath; when Mum did the washing, she had to remove the frogs.'

'We had asparagus fern — but why no asparagus? It had an interesting smell about it. Didn't seem to be really real — a weed fern. We used to dig it up looking for asparagus, but there was none there.'

'Magpies. Couldn't go out the back in the nesting season without a piece of wood. Beautiful singers. Liquid notes. Gorgeous. Lots of birds. Kookaburras...'

2 Start with a Tree to Climb

The sheer pleasure of a low limb on the nature strip

Kids adore trees — and they know immediately whether a tree is climbable or not. A tree has to have a number of special characteristics to be a good climb. The perfect children's climbing tree has: a short sturdy trunk, strong low branches, a wide spreading habit, smooth non-scratchy bark, a good dense leaf cover. Secondary characteristics which are desirable but not essential are: soft grassy ground beneath so children can jump down without being hurt; low branches from which they can swing on their hands; a location that gives access to important places like the shed roof or the neighbour's fruit tree; a position that gives the climber a good view over interesting things happening all around (on the nature strip outside the fence is excellent).

For many of us who don't have the space or time to grow huge trees, a nearby park can be a good alternative, but if you would like to grow a climbing tree in your garden, the trees in this chapter have been chosen to suit both the gardener who wants an attractive garden and the child who wants to climb. Four main criteria governed their selection:

'The children's tree', Royal Botanic Gardens, Sydney (*Ficus macrophylla*)

Strictly a park treat, the Moreton Bay fig is the king of all Australian climbing trees: buttressed so that children can practically walk up into it, spreading vast strong branches that they could sleep overnight in, notched with interesting hiding nooks round its base and often throwing down strong aerial roots from which kids can swing like Tarzan. Native to New South Wales and Queensland, this majestic tree is excruciatingly slow growing, so even if you did have a garden big enough to take one, it wouldn't be ready for climbing for many generations, but it rivals England's oak in every way.

- They are all fast-growing so they will be just about big enough by the time your children are, provided you plant when the first one is born ... but don't expect miracles — it takes a long time to grow a tree.
- They don't object to being transplanted at a mature size so you can start off with a good big advanced plant.
- They have safe non-brittle branches.
- They each have at least one outstanding feature — blossoms, coloured leaves, a graceful shape, an unusual habit — which alone will justify their place in the garden.

How to help a tree grow into a good climbing tree

1 Make sure you select a species that suits your climate, otherwise it will never thrive. No matter how much you admire a beautiful silver birch in Bowral, it will always look spindly and unwell in Sydney's sub-tropical beach suburbs.
2 Make sure you choose a good, well-branched specimen from the nursery.
3 Plant in full all-day sun so the tree can relax and spread out its branches instead of having to stretch up for light.
4 Water and fertilise regularly so it gets no setbacks.
5 Leave plenty of space around the tree so it can spread without feeling crowded; in the centre of the lawn is best.
6 Consider cutting the top out of a young plant to encourage low branching, but consult your nurseryman on purchase before doing this.

Good Climbs in Everyday Trees

Peppercorn tree (*Schinus molle*). One of the best trees to climb for several reasons. The thick round irregular limbs originate very low on the short stocky trunk. Branches are covered with a pleasant-textured bark. A lacy tracery of feathery foliage, often weeping to the ground,

Plant a pepper tree (*Schinus molle*) for the featheriest, laciest climb of all

gives a light airy feel to the inside of the tree. It is a good safe tree with a very deep strong root system. One big advantage for a young family is that it is an extremely rapid grower. Peppers perform splendidly in hot dry places as well as in cooler climates and are especially good for hard adverse conditions. Attractive clusters of pink-red berries are excellent for harmless throwing games while crushed leaves smell pleasantly of pepper. Originally from South Africa, it will live for fifty years. One slight disadvantage is that the spring flowers can be irritating to allergic or asthmatic children. Grows to 10 metres. Suitable for all climates except the really cold.

Jacaranda (*Jacaranda mimosifolia*) This lovely flowering tree has everything a climber needs: short, rarely-straight stem, strong rounded main branches commencing low on the trunk, pleasantly textured smooth bark and a cool green foliage cover in the long summer holidays. A special attraction is that for three weeks in spring (often coinciding with exam time in

Already a good climb: a young jacaranda in full bloom on the nature strip

Australian schools) climbing can be done in a blue haze when the jacaranda, briefly deciduous, puts out a mass of flowers before the summer foliage. A fast grower. Very frost sensitive when young. Advanced plants will transplant exceptionally well. The only drawback for climbing is that some terminal branches are a little brittle. Very variable in habit but generally growing to 12 metres. Grows in all climates except very cold.

London Plane (*Platanus* x *acerifolia*) Provided a couple of pieces of wood are nailed to the trunk for access, the London plane makes a great climb: totally hardy, extremely strong branches,

Rich grandfathers could present a plane tree this size to a newborn grandchild

17

fast growing and with a dense summer leaf cover that makes it a wonderful hideout tree as well as providing good shade. Moreover, it has an attractive mottled bark and good seed pods for attacking trespassers. Particularly suitable for city gardens as it withstands smog, heat, shade, cold and car fumes; however, it needs a good big space to spread as it often stretches 10 metres wide. One of the great assets of the plane is that it will take transplanting in its stride even at the advanced size of 5 metres, so you could almost have an instant climb. Grows to 15 metres. Not suitable for tropics.

A mature plane perfectly placed as a look-out tree

Horse chestnut (*Aesculus hippocastanum*) One of the chief attractions of this tree for children is that, having climbed the thick vertical trunk and reached the cover of the dense foliage, they have access to the large, tough-skinned fruit containing the lustrous brown conkers which they can rain down in autumn on their passing friends. Deciduous, fast growing, very long lived, the horse chestnut appeals to adults too by producing in spring big spikes of white flowers, giving the tree the effect of being decorated with white candles. A fine tree with a tall domed crown, it grows well in most climates but must

have moisture. Drought can be very damaging but it withstands wind well. Interestingly, the wood is occasionally used for making children's toys. Advanced plants lift well. Height to 12 metres. Not suitable for the tropics.

Indian Bean (*Catalpa bignonoides*) Surprisingly, the beautiful, strong limbed *Catalpa* — not tall, but spreading widely — is not planted extensively in New South Wales but it makes a superb flowering tree for children to climb with its stout, pale brown trunk and graceful branches forking out broadly from near ground level, the branch tips of mature trees often sweeping the ground elegantly. Fast growing with wonderful big heart-shaped leaves and large clusters of fragrant foxglove-like flowers in white, pink or lemon, followed by dangling pods like cigars. A native of the Mississippi Valley, it is pest-free, tolerates smog, but, though it likes a slightly cooler climate, is frost tender. The only problem for children is that its leaves have a rather unpleasant smell when crushed. Large specimens can be transplanted. Not suitable for tropics. Height to 15 metres with a spread to 8 metres.

Japanese Maple (*Acer palmatum*) A particularly good climbing tree for very young children in cooler districts because the bark is silky smooth, slim branches fork very low to the ground, limbs emerge very frequently and regularly from the trunk and the whole tree rarely grows higher than 6 metres. Pale green long-fingered leaves

The Japanese maple is a gentle friendly climb for very young children

create a wonderful dappled translucent hideaway in summer, while the autumn colours are red, scarlet and gold. Deciduous. A fast grower. To 6 metres. Not suitable for the tropics or for older children.

Liquidambar (*Liquidambar styraciflua; L. formosana*) An advanced plant of this beautiful tree, if planted when the child is born, will be ready to climb by its fourth birthday. Regularly placed branches starting very low on the strong central stem make it an excellent climb for younger children, yet it grows big enough to suit older children too. Star-shaped leaves are its special glory, budding a pale translucent green in spring and turning an incredible range of colours in autumn — pink, gold, purple, black, scarlet, orange. This pyramidal tree makes a spectacular lawn specimen and is one of the really long-lived trees, lasting eight generations of children. Likes moisture. Autumn foliage is best where there are cooler winters but grows anywhere except the tropics. Oils extracted from its bark are used in chewing gum. A greedy feeder. Grows to about 12 metres.

Camphor laurel (*Cinnamomum camphora*) Not as fast-growing as others mentioned, the camphor laurel will take longer to become a really good climb as young camphor laurels are a bit upright to begin with. At its mature best, however, it is a wonderful climbing tree, with a short massive trunk, thick upright branches and huge spreading crown. One of its chief attractions is its soft apple-green spring foliage which, when it drops later in autumn, makes a beautifully fragrant fire. In fact, the smell of camphor is given off by any broken parts of this tree, while the volatile oils are attractive to butterflies. It is also attractive to currawongs when the inconspicuous fruit is ripe. A native of Japan, the camphor laurel provides a challenging climb for older children, very strong and safe, with silky-feeling, deeply furrowed bark. Rarely seen in nurseries, however, and considered by some a pest for invading natural bush. Grows to 20 metres.

Magnolia (*Magnolia grandiflora*) If you want a huge tree to be ready for your grandchildren to climb, with solid branches like walkways, this is it: the queen of flowering trees with its dark green lacquered leaves and huge dinner-plate sized waxen white flowers and smooth massive boughs. Not suitable for small gardens as the massive branches fork low and spread wide, but very hardy and resistant to pollution. It grows beautifully in Sydney, coastal districts and anywhere warm including the tropics but is rather slower growing than some of the others mentioned in this chaper. Children carve the huge, tightly-packed buds with a pocket-knife. Can grow to 25 metres, though usually less. A very widely spreading tree.

Huge old camphor laurel: a wonderful climb if you're lucky enough to own one

The fat bud of the magnolia

Norway Maple (*Acer platanoides*) Not only do the powerful spreading well-spaced limbs and sturdy trunk of this tall tree make a great climb, but it produces winged V-shaped green seeds which flutter to the ground like little helicopters if twirled by small fingers. Children also love the five-lobed leaves which are coppery red in new growth, green in summer, primrose in autumn. Easily transplanted at advanced size. The Norway maple is utterly hardy, thrives in almost any soil and withstands moderate coastal exposure. Smooth dark grey bark, yellow flowers. A fast grower in the early stages, it will eventually attain 20 metres.

Golden Rain Tree (*Koelreuteria paniculata*) An unusual dome-shaped deciduous tree producing big sprays of yellow flowers in spring followed by even more showy sprays of papery bladder-like seed pods in a reddish-pink that persist for months. A good tree for climbing because its strong, low, rounded branches, which often give the tree a picturesque shape when young, emerge low on the trunk. One of the best trees for strongly alkaline soils, though badly affected by wind. A fast-growing tree that does well in cooler districts, but also well in Sydney. It likes sun and shelter to flourish. Not suitable for tropics. Grows to about 10 metres.

Tulip Tree (*Liriodendron tulipifera*) If the middle is cut out when young, the side branches of this lovely deciduous tree will be encouraged and it will grow to an excellent climbing tree, retaining branches to ground level. Closely related to magnolias, the flowers are a beautiful tulip-shaped chartreuse and orange, though carried a bit too high to matter. Best in cooler districts. A fast grower from North America with large

The curiously shaped leaf of the tulip tree turns gold in autumn

leaves that turn yellow in autumn. Not for tropics or small gardens. Grows to 25 metres.

Californian Strawberry Tree (*Arbutus menziesii*) Sometimes called Madrone. Not to be confused with the much smaller, bushy, Irish strawberry tree, this attractive ornamental with large trunk, unusual peeling bark, gnarled limbs and smooth orange-red fruit makes a great small climbing tree with good horizontal branching and should be planted more in New South Wales. Often multi-stemmed, it makes an attractive flower display in spring. Grows very well in Canberra. Very good small tree for dry conditions. It is not often seen in nurseries, however, because it is a bit temperamental about being transplanted. An unusual and interesting tree that grows to 12 metres given the right spot.

Virgilia (*Virgilia oroboides*, formerly *capensis*) A small, dense, shrubby, extremely fast-growing tree that will suit very young children to climb while waiting for a more substantial tree to mature. In spring its rather light twiggy branches can be a picture, covered with very conspicuous pinky mauve pea-like flowers and rather delicate, fern-like green foliage. Frequently used as a street tree in Sydney, *Virgilia* would never be substantial enough for older children to climb. Short-lived. Shallow-rooted. Grows at rate of 2 metres or more a year — quite phenomenal. Grows to about 6 metres in height, spreading to 4 metres.

Sweet or Spanish Chestnut (*Castanea sativa*) A gorgeous huge spreading tree, stretching almost as wide as it is high, the chestnut is one of the world's most wonderful climbing trees, though fortunately not as slow as the oaks, beeches, elms and other climbing trees associated with the woods and parks of England. Very long-lived. Deciduous, providing wonderful summer shade, the tree produces edible chestnuts which children can roast over the open fire in a perforated pan though collecting the nuts daily during leaf fall is almost as much fun as eating them (gloves are needed for those with burrs still on). Great for country gardens, the chestnut grows quite fast to 10 metres, then more slowly to its full majestic height. Needs a good rainfall. Will bear in three to ten years. Not suitable for tropics. Grows to over 20 metres.

Carob or Locust Tree (*Ceratonia siliqua*) A dense dark evergreen domed tree, very compact, with attractive and interesting crooked branches which provide a safe climb for younger children. Originally from the Mediterranean, it thrives in very dry conditions, throwing a heavy summer shade. It also tolerates smog well. A true survival tree, it will produce a crop of sugary bean pods in the fourth year of total drought. The pods are sweet and chocolate brown and are used to produce a chocolate substitute. Seeds were used historically as the original carat weight.

Kaffir Plum (*Harpephyllum caffrum*) The best thing about this tree is the array of massive branches radiating in a great circle from the stout cylindrical trunk. The branches are as round and smooth and grey as an elephant's trunk, beautifully smooth to climb. A tree with

A comforting tree to climb: the kaffir plum, this one with a perfectly placed sandpile to jump into

a wonderful dense dark canopy to sit amongst, forming a round-headed crown, but throwing such a dense shade nothing will grow under it. An excellent climbing tree, it grows beautifully in Sydney, often being used as a street tree. Fruits are edible, rose pink and make delicious jam. Fast growing. Grows to 10 metres.

Lime or Linden (*Tilia* x *vulgaris*) A mature lime is one of the great climbing trees with its lower branches arching downwards and then turning up at the ends, a short, heavily-buttressed trunk and the ascending branches forming a beautifully shaped high rounded crown. The grey bark is smooth and comfortable and it tolerates very hard wear. Delicate lime-green leaves are heart-shaped. Deciduous. Tolerates smog and is a popular tree in Sydney's parks, though it grows faster in slightly cooler districts. The wood of lime trees is used for making piano keys. A good fast grower in a moist climate. To 20 metres.

Poinciana (*Delonix regia*) Though this tree is not a particularly fast grower, it is such a popular climbing tree in Queensland and other warm areas that it is worth planting for the next generation of kids to enjoy … or worth buying a house with a mature one in its garden. A graceful, broad-domed tree forming a wonderful canopy: light green leaves give it a delicate, fern-like appearance while for two months in summer it is covered in large bright red-orange flowers. Must have plenty of space for its deep spreading roots to develop. Grows to 15 x 8 metres.

Dragon Tree (*Dracaena draco*) This rare and dramatic tree from the Canary Islands is available in Sydney nurseries, though most children are more familiar with it from the Royal Botanic Gardens in Sydney where a superb specimen has been climbed in by generations of four-year-olds. It forms a natural nook deep within, thoroughly enclosed, with a smooth soft sitting space and a dim spooky light — yet the child is no more than a metre off the ground. Its thickened sap is said to be dragon's blood. A moderately fast grower, wider than it is tall. To 4 metres. See colour plates on page 30.

Golden Poplar (*Populus* x *canadensis* 'Aurea') A very fast growing deciduous tree with shiny lemon yellow foliage turning deep gold in autumn: a beautiful sight shimmering in full sun and a good sturdy climb. Not a suitable tree for city gardens, however, as the invasive roots choke drains. Not to be confused with the tall columnar Lombardy poplar.

Australian Eucalypts that give safe climbing

Imagine clambering around on these smooth grey eucalypt limbs

Eucalypts look especially right in Australian home gardens, but many species not only have a bad reputation for dropping branches, but are so erratic in habit that there is a certain amount of pot luck in producing one that will be a great climb. The eucalypts included here have been vetted for safe climbing. Interestingly, eucalypts do not grow faster from an advanced plant. It is better to buy a young seedling which will romp away immediately than to ride out the setback to an advanced specimen caused by transplanting.

Red Bloodwood (*Eucalyptus gummifera*) A good fast growing gum, well shaped for climbing with spreading branches and a strong trunk. It produces abundant strongly-scented cream flowers in large clusters. Red bloodwoods have the added attraction (for children) of exuding from wounds on trunk and branches a red gum called 'kino' which children love to play with. Grows well on poor soils, clay or sand. 15 to 30 metres tall, but can get too narrow and elongated for climbing if not given enough space to spread.

Tuart (*Eucalyptus gomphocephala*) An excellent climbing tree, fast growing, very low branching

and densely foliated so it provides both privacy and shade. Light grey fibrous bark. Attractive to birds, particularly when white flowers are in bloom from January to March. From Western Australia originally, it likes lime. Useful for coastal planting as it tolerates salinity. Spreads very wide to 20 metres if given space. Can grow to 30 metres.

Sydney Red Gum (*Angophora costata*) This would be a good shaped climbing tree for the first 15 years when it is still pyramidal, then later a swing could be strung from its twisted, gnarled and spreading matured branches. One of the most magnificently coloured trunks of all our gum trees — a delicate pink, shading to green, red and orange, very smooth to the touch, dimpled. Fast growing. Bird attracting. Particularly useful because it grows in poor soils. It occurs naturally in the Sydney district where it is treasured by those lucky enough to have a mature tree. Grows to 20 metres.

Snow Gum (*Eucalyptus pauciflora*) A climbing tree for cooler areas. Wonderful crooked stems with gleaming smooth white or cream bark, dappled with pale pink and grey and usually marked with scribbles from insect larvae. This

The contorted limbs of the snow gum offer a great climb

picturesque tree with its dense round crown and spreading branches is a good safe tree that can weep to the ground in some forms. Not to be grown in hot conditions as it gets stressed. Moderately fast growing. Will grow to 20 metres.

Bangalay (*Eucalyptus botryoides*) Along with the Blackbutt and *E. grandis*, this is eventually far too immense and columnar a tree for city gardens. However, all three grow so astonishingly fast they make great temporary climbing trees while waiting for others to grow, after which they could be cut down. It is also one of the most adaptable of gums, growing well in many conditions including salt spray and heavy wind, hanging on well in sand and poorly

drained soils. Koalas eat its gum tips. Widely spreading with a fairly dense crown. In a good situation this is an enormous tree, but when exposed to strong saline coastal winds is smaller and shrubbier in appearance.

Swamp Bloodwood (*Eucalyptus ptychocarpa*) This is a spectacular tree at flowering time (March): the blooms drip nectar which attracts birds of every kind, especially honey eaters. Quite a fast growing erect tree with a stout stem, dense crown and widely spreading branches, it flourishes everywhere given warm days, water and sunshine. Bark is grey and fibrous but not uncomfortable to climb. Very attractive big nuts. Much more reliable for sub-tropical climates than the Western Australian red flowering gum. Grows to 12 or 14 metres.

Swamp Mahogany (*Eucalyptus robusta*) One of the rare densely-leaved gums, robusta has a crown thick enough to give privacy to the climber. A very tough, hardy tree, it grows well in severely exposed conditions, wind, even swamps, remaining nice and sturdy. Its gum tips are attractive to koalas. Fast growing. Likes water. Two disadvantages: a rather rough bark, and often marred by leaf lerp infestation in Sydney area. Grows to 18 metres.

Climb Patriotically in Australian Native Trees

Cedar Wattle (*Acacia elata*) An outstanding, fast growing, unusually long-lived wattle suitable for all children to climb (providing they don't have asthma). Branches very spreading and low to ground. Bark is smooth. Creamy wattle balls, very fluffy, which appear in dense profuse clusters in summer. A lovely lawn tree, suitable for light to medium moist soil. Deep green ferny foliage. Very hardy. Can grow to 16 metres, but rarely reaches this in cultivation.

Blackwood (*Acacia melanoxylon*) An excellent climbing tree branching right from the ground

Playing in a lightning-struck *Acacia .elata*

23

into a symmetrical dense crown of evergreen foliage, producing pale yellow flower balls in winter. Very fast-growing yet, unusually for wattles, long-lived. Wind resistant. Frost resistant. Very hardy. Tolerates wet feet. Altogether an excellent wattle which should be more widely grown. Children like the quaintly twisted pods which sometimes curl round into a full circle. When grown as a solitary specimen, this outstanding tree will spread its pendulous branches to 9 metres. Likes moisture. The Aborigines used the roasted bark to make a hot infusion to bathe rheumatic joints. Will grow to 20 metres in good conditions. Acacias grow better from seed.

Paperbark (*Melaleuca quinquenervia*) A bit unpredictable in habit, but at its best a wonderful low-branching spreading tree for children to climb, its chief attraction being the soft, thick, pliable bark which can be peeled off in multi-layered sheets and is wonderfully soft to climb. Bird attracting. Fast growing. Loves wet feet. Tolerates brackish conditions, salt spray, strong winds. Occasionally a bit too upright and lacking low branches, but if cut out in the middle when young, will tend to branch, especially if grown in an uncrowded position. A particularly fine stand of climbable paperbarks can be seen in Sydney's Centennial Park from Lang Road. Grows to 15 metres.

This splendid climb is a mature *Melaleuca quinquenervia*

Brush Box (*Lophostemon confertus* syn. *Tristania conferta*) An excellent climbing tree, extremely hardy, with a strong straight stem and sturdy branches. Very fast growing in the early stages, it provides a dense green crown that allows the climber complete privacy. The only disadvantage is some rough bark at the butt, but that could be viewed as a challenge. The chief advantage is that the tree is almost totally pest free, will fend for itself completely in most soils and will also stand up to abuse. Has been used extensively for street planting in Sydney, but is often badly misshapen from pruning. If the branches start a bit high from the ground, a few pieces of board nailed to the trunk will do the tree no harm. To 40 metres. *Tristaniopsis laurina* syn. *T. laurina* is a smaller version, growing to only about 7 metres, frequently with several trunks.

Port Jackson Fig (*Ficus rubiginosa*) and **Small-fruited Fig** (*F. hillii*). These are the two figs that make Sydney's streets a tree-climbing paradise for children. Fast growing. Incredibly adaptable. They have all that makes a good climbing tree: low branches, strong, thick and rounded; a smooth light bark; dense attractive green foliage.

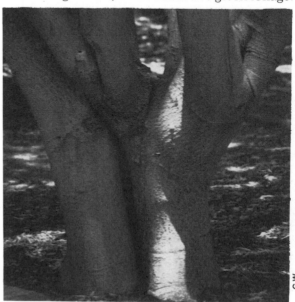

The sturdy grey limbs of the Sydney fig are familiar to generations of Sydney children

Practically indestructible. Heavy pruning has spoiled the shape of many street trees, but left to grow develops a large spreading attractive shape, though not as massive as the Moreton Bay Fig. A bit messy at fruiting time. Attractive to fruit bats. Rubiginosa grows to 20 metres, hillii to 15 metres.

Willow Myrtle (*Agonis flexuosa*) A good native tree for small gardens and small children. Slender when young, with grey-green willow-like weeping branches from a short trunk, it can grow into quite a thick gnarled stocky tree with a dense crown. The rough furrowed brown bark is not unpleasant to the skin. In spring and summer, numerous tiny white flowers seem to cover the leaf stalks. It is an excellent small tree for a dry garden, extremely hardy, and takes a lot of punishment. Wide spreading in relation to its size, it is often seen in Sydney gardens. It rarely reaches its maximum height of 12 metres.

Fruit Trees — Eat while you climb

Children have traditionally climbed fruit trees: it is one of the joys of being young. The fruit trees listed here have been selected as reasonably fast-growing, suitable for the home garden, less attractive to fruit fly than some and of a suitable habit for climbing. Do not bother planting exotic fruits if you want to please children. Children are normally such conservative eaters they tend to rear back at the sight of a feijoa, a carambola or a lychee.

Mulberry (*Morus alba*) This is perhaps one of the all-time great children's trees. An outstandingly fast grower. Small enough for city gardens. Wonderful gnarled, rugged shape perfect for climbing. Tough enough to stand almost anything — destructive kids, polluted air, stony soil, shade, total neglect. Pest free. Produces huge crops of mulberries each spring which are almost universally liked by children. And as the final bonus: mulberry leaves are food for all those shoe-boxes full of silkworms that primary school children are so devoted to. Best of all, the mulberry will thrive literally anywhere; just throw a few mulberries on the ground next spring in the general direction of where you want a tree, and shortly you'll have one. Chopping out the head encourages lower shoots. Birds are very fond of the fruit. Mulberry stains on children's clothing can be removed by rubbing with a green mulberry (or so they say). Numerous horticultural varieties available. Not suitable for cold climates with heavy frosts. Grows to 10 metres.

Apricot (*Prunus armeniaca*) Good bearing trees for the home garden, apricots, native to Asia, will grow in almost any climate except one with severe spring frosts (though they prefer a cool winter). The ideal fruiting shape to aim for is a tree with a short stout trunk and branches spreading obliquely outwards, which is just the right shape for climbing too. Branches may occasionally be a little brittle, but as apricots are not tall growers, they are quite safe. Apricots fruit particularly well in the Sydney district and, because they crop earlier than peaches and cherries, avoid the worst of the fruit fly though a Dak Pot or similar is advisable. The most important point if you want an apricot tree for climbing as well as fruit is to tell the nurseryman you do *not* want a grafted plant, because many apricots are grafted on to dwarf stock. Apricots will start bearing in three to four years and remain productive for forty years. A bushy tree to 5 metres.

Pear (*Pyrus communis*) An excellent fruit tree for districts with cold winters. Pears crop in winter thus avoiding the worst of the fruit fly.

An heirloom tree: the pear

Encouragement of lateral branches is not only essential for a good crop but creates the perfect shape for climbing too. Make sure you purchase one that has not been grafted on to dwarf stock. Pears will attain 20 metres and last three hundred years, but buy a grafted tree because seedling trees may take eighty years to bear!

A beautiful ornamental pear tree for climbing would be the Manchurian pear (not the spiny Chinese one) which, though it doesn't fruit, is a remarkably fast growing tree with a stout vertical trunk, strong angular upright branches and wonderful autumn leaf colours.

Mango (*Mangifera indica*) Mangoes make magnificent climbing trees in tropical districts with their dense crown giving welcome shade, heavy crops of luscious fruit and attractive dark green appearance. They are an excellent shape for climbing with easy access via a short stout trunk to a maze of crowded branches. Must have ample water and a good rich soil but, given that, will even crop well in Sydney if planted in a warm sheltered winter aspect. If the mango tree needs a few boards nailed to the trunk for access so much the better, because galvanised iron nails are said to encourage heavy cropping.

Fig (*Ficus carica*) Everyone who used to climb an eating fig tree when young remembers the flexible branches with affection. Possibly the reason why the actual fruit is remembered less often is that the birds and the fruit fly got to it first. A deciduous tree of the mulberry family,

the fig is adaptable to a wide range of climates from cool temperate to sub-tropical and bears after just four years. The flowers are borne inside the fruit which is actually a swollen flower stalk. Pollination is carried out by the female fig wasp, after which plastic bags can be tied round fruit to prevent marauders. A very good backyard climb.

Walnut (*Juglans regia*) If you live in a large garden and have a cold winter, the spreading crown and zig-zag lower branches of this noble tree make for wonderful climbing. Called the English or Persian walnut, it is not only quite a fast grower but will bear nuts in five to eight years. A deep-rooted tree not suitable for sandy shallow soil. To 10 metres but spreads to more than its height.

Olive (*Olea europaea*) Curiously, many children love the sour taste of olives and as a climbing tree they are excellent: evergreen, very hardy, will survive in dry conditions and grow quickly to 6 metres. In time, their grey trunks become gnarled and picturesque in appearance. The olive grows well in most areas in Australia — tropics to temperate — will thrive in most soils and is almost free of disease and pest.

In a big country garden, this young oak tree would be an investment for the future, but oaks are far too slow-growing to be of use to the present generation of climbers

Tree Accessories

Children love stuff hanging about on trees. Frayed knotted ropes. Old tyres. A sandpit full of plastic ice-cream containers nestling between the roots. However, beauty is in the eye of the

This brush box on the nature strip seems to survive despite the dangling ropes and other impedimenta

beholder and while these tree accessories may look charmingly homey to some families, others believe they impart to the garden a quite astonishing air of squalour. Some comfort can be taken concerning sandpits, — often little else will grow under trees *except* sandpits — but in the general matter of tree accessories, a few that are rather less offensive than most are listed below.

The hammock. If you have two trees handily placed, children of all ages love hammocks. The best sort to buy for children is the camping-type hammock in jungle green net that is fairly cheap and can stay out in all weathers. Being green it blends in with the garden unobtrusively. However, if you are prepared to move them in at night, there are picturesque ones made of cotton with fringes and cushions that give the garden a delicious air of summery repose.

The rope ladder. Hung from a low branch, the rope ladder gives young children a lot of fun without looking too hopelessly untidy. They are usually quite short, sturdy and not unattractive. Purchase from kindergarten supply stores.

The basketball hoop. A ring of iron nailed to the tree gives hours of pleasure to older children in the garden. If craftily placed by the gardener there's every chance the hoop will be almost totally concealed, but the scuffed lawn underneath it during the basketball season may be a giveaway.

The tree house. This is the ultimate tree accessory in children's minds: a place of their own far from adult eyes. Tree houses can range in splendour

Tree houses range from a few bits and pieces balanced rakishly across a branch......to a verandahed bungalow with electric light

27

'Single story. Close to shops and transport. Extensive views. Northerly aspect. Light and sunny. Easy access. Many safety features. Big garden. Vacant possession.'

Parents have a lot of fun building them

A fast exit via a fireman's pole

from a few pieces of fruit-box nailed to the branch by the local kids to a magnificent construction sawed to precise specifications by an engineering father. The following aspects are the really important ones.

1 The platform of the tree house should ideally be flat, firm and steady.

2 The house should (ideally) be roomy enough to *do* things up there.

3 A really excellent tree house goes right round the tree.

4 A circuitous access route is interesting.

5 Ease of access is sometimes desirable, sometimes not, depending on whether you want to keep other people out.

6 Interesting tree houses are ones with two stories, annexes or crow's nests.

7 Any tree house is better than no tree house. Even a single board across a low fork fits the fond description — 'my tree house'.

Last but not least — the swing. Since you won't wriggle out of providing a swing for the children if you have any sort of substantial tree, you might as well just make the best of it and hope the most suitable branch from which to hang it isn't in the centre of your most precious stretch of lawn. Opt

Most gardens can produce a handy branch on which to hang a swing...

Children love a garden full of interesting 'places' and levels

Children love feeding the fish

Fences are fun to climb

Most parents can rig up a swing of sorts......but a hanging rope will do, especially when there's a low stump to jump off

G.W.

Four year olds' favourite: the dragon tree (page 21)

for safety first: an old car tyre is ideal for small children because it is so much safer than a wooden seat if pushed without an occupant. Other options include a T-bar type arrangement with a rope and rod, a canvas sling or various rather gaudy manufactured plastic animal arrangements. And if your garden just doesn't boast the appropriate tree, you'll have to fall back on the manufactured metal-framed swing, or better, one with a frame made of treated pine, or even one you make yourself.

Trees for Other Purposes

Climbing them and using them for tree houses are not the only uses children find for trees. There are many individual trees treasured by Australian children for special characteristics in their own right — perhaps for the seed pods they produce, their smell or for the fact that their leaves make good harmonicas. Some universal favourites include:

Weeping Willow (*Salix babylonica*) Just about every child loves a willow tree, not only for the way it looks, but for the way it forms a green cubby underneath screened off by long green curtains. Unfortunately, particularly in cities,

Willow trees make a green-walled cubby

willows have a reputation as the villain of the piece, their aggressive roots clogging and splitting sewer pipes, their extremely rapid growth and huge size soon overextending their allotted spot. Willows are possibly the easiest tree to grow of all, striking easily from any sized

cutting … and most willows have twisted and contorted branches that are good for climbing too. As an added interest, it is the wood of the willow that is used to make cricket bats. Very fast growing. Grows anywhere provided it is given plenty of water. To 15 metres.

Pine Trees Principally loved for the soft forest-like floor that accumulates underneath due to the dropping of the needles — a sweet-smelling gentle place to play. Handfuls of pine needles

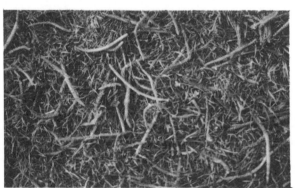
Pine needles are so satisfying to strip

can be used for making everything from bird's nests to fairy beds. Added attractions of the pine family are pine cones (which are fun to collect and which burn in the fire with a wonderful red glow), pine needles (which are very satisfactory to strip) and the sticky gum which exudes from wounds in the tree. Generally speaking, they are not good climbing trees because the bark is very rough and scaly, though there is some disagreement on this:

31

'We lived in a big country town and there was a grove of huge old pine trees just near our side fence. Someone had once lopped off one of the pines at about 20 feet (5 metres) though it seemed about 80 feet (25 metres) to us, and the branches had grown out sideways leaving a natural bower. We played up in that tree every summer. We didn't mind the scratchy bark: it kept out invaders'.

Trees with Long Tall Trunks Trees whose branches don't start until well above ground are considered a highly desirable garden asset by children. Tree tiggy, hide and seek, backyard

Children love trees with long tall trunks

cricket and all games like thunder and lightning are played under these trees. They are also useful for nailing things on like dart boards, catherine wheels, tail-on-the-donkey games. Of course, a collection of these columnar trees is even better, especially for playing tree-to-tree or hidings. An excellent tree of this type that comes to mind is the lemon-scented gum (*Eucalyptus citriodora*) which has the added attraction of giving off a wonderful lemon smell when the mower runs over the fallen leaves.

A favourite: the silvery catkins of the pussy willow

Pussy Willow (*Salix caprea*) The pussy willow tree is such an all-time favourite with children that it has been immortalised in a poem called 'Have you ever seen a pussy in a pussy willow tree?' In early spring, the bare brown branches sprout shining silky silver catkins that feel like velvet. On the whole, adults find it rather an unattractive invasive plant in the garden, aggressively working its roots towards water and drains, but if you have a damp isolated spot, perhaps it is worth a place. A short suckering deciduous tree, it will grow very easily and quickly from large cuttings. Just let the cutting soak in a bucket until roots appear. Grows in virtually any climate except tropical.

She-Oaks (*Casuarina* species) These are great trees to doodle with: the dried needles break into such neat little segments that children can sit for hours just breaking off pieces. Actually the needles are not leaves but adapted stalks; the

Casuarina needles snap into neat satisfying segments

little teeth at the end of each segment are the leaves. A decorative small tree giving a nice Australian flavour to the garden, often with interesting bark or patterned seedpods that can be used to mark the edges of pastry for pies. Many species for all situations, even ones that turn into good climbing trees. Casuarina trees make a wonderful carpet underneath like pine trees.

Casuarina trees drop a soft carpet

Maple Trees (*Acer* species) In autumn, every tree of the maple family produces millions of little green helicopters with aerodynamically

The winged seed of the maple spins like a helicopter rotor

designed wing blades. Children like to climb the tree, twirl the seed stalk between thumb and finger and watch squadrons of miniature helicopters descend to a landing.

Spinning Gum (*Eucalyptus crucis*) The silvery juvenile leaves of this dainty eucalyptus grow opposite each other on the stem, but are completely joined. The leaves, as they die, become detached from the stem and form discs which spin in the wind — or can be spun — with a satisfying rattly sound. Quick growing, this is a very hardy small tree with a dainty twisted habit and beautiful grey-green foliage.

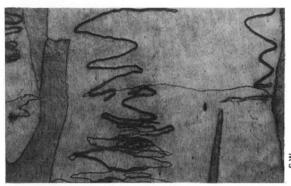

The dead leaves of the spinning gum can be spun on their stalks

Withstands wet soil which is unusual for a gum. Makes wonderful cut foliage.

Scribbly Gum (*Eucalyptus haemastoma*) It is the interesting scribbles drawn on the white trunks

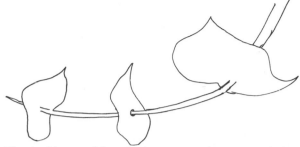

Children love the smooth bark and strange markings of the scribbly gum

and branches of the scribbly gum that attracts children. The scribbles are actually made by the larvae of an insect and get thicker as the insect gets bigger. But even apart from the scribbles this is an interesting tree for children with its twisted gnarled shape and its beautifully tinted pale trunk, especially as the gum tips are koala food. Scribbly gums grow well on shallow Hawkesbury sandstone soils but are fairly slow and it might be necessary to check the branches periodically for stability.

African Tulip Tree (*Spathodea campanulata*) The fat orange-scarlet flower buds of this large evergreen tree contain enough liquid to send out disconcerting jets when pricked with a pin and squeezed, hence its alternate name of Fountain Tree. It even has a third popular name — Sorcerer's Wand Tree — because the flowers cluster on the end of long straight branches reminiscent of the red handkerchiefs that pop

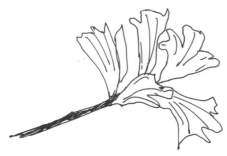

The magician's wand unfurls (flowers of the African Tulip Tree)

from the end of magician's canes. But not a good climbing tree because the branches are very brittle. Flowers for two months in summer. A handsome tree for large gardens. Needs a frost-free situation. Grows to 17 metres.

Paperbark (*Melaleuca quinquenervia*) The soft dry sheets of bark that this tree produces are so satisfyingly layered, film upon film, and present so many jagged edges, and peel back to reveal so many subtle shades of colour, that children can't seem to resist pulling it off — and in moderation it doesn't seem to harm the tree. Whether they actually use it for paper or not is questionable, but it is certainly useful for lining cubby houses, making bark pictures, etc. One of the few Australian native trees that likes wet feet. Attractive to birds. Grows to about 20 metres.

The unusual layered bark of the paperbark tree (*Melaleuca quinquenervia*)

3 There's No Substitute for a Lawn

With children about, you need a lawn. A flat sunny lawn can virtually give you an extra (outdoor) room. But with children about, there is no chance of growing a velvety sward — so don't even attempt it. Compromise is the only solution. A lawn for children must be comfortable enough to sit on and lie down on, but tough enough to stand up to tricycles, chasings, handstands and fireworks night. In other words, with children in the family, you settle for a utility lawn.

Lawns come in all shapes and sizes

Selecting the Right Grass

By choosing the right sort of grass and using commonsense in its maintenance, the gardener and the child can (almost) learn to live together with the lawn.

Buffalo Grass (*Stenotaphrum secundatum*) Whatever you do, don't be talked into planting this extremely hardy grass. Although it is the very best of grasses for taking foot traffic and although it resists most known grass diseases, children universally loathe it. It not only itches

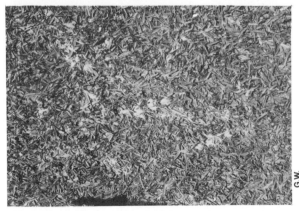

About the only good thing buffalo grass has going for it is that its spongy habit cushions falls in tag football

35

tender skin, but the coarse blunt leaves are almost prickly, they are so scratchy. It forms a lawn that has a sort of hostile toughness that is the opposite of inviting. The colour too is far from lush: a sort of grey green with whitish runners showing through, it tends to invade garden beds badly. Its one advantage is that it resists bindii. Usually the most expensive turf sold commercially, buffalo lawn has its place (which might be as a lawn whose spongey springy toughness takes a game of tag football or badminton), but as the main lawn for young children — no.

Common Couch (*Cynodon dactylon*) This, on the other hand, is still the best, all-round, backyard lawn for Australia's children to play on. It is a soft, fine-leaved utility grass which creates a pleasant carpet-like effect, yet the tough strong leaves do not bruise easily. It stays soft and green even in dry weather. It is extremely wear resistant. It is easily established and adaptable to a wide range of soil conditions. It is resistant to most diseases. The only disadvantages of a couch lawn are that it tends to brown off a little in winter and it can only flourish in full sun. Common couch is widely distributed throughout the warm and hot parts of the world, tolerates sea spray, tolerates close mowing, recovers extremely quickly after drought. It can be planted from seed readily available from all garden stores or by ordering turf.

Nurserymen are constantly trying various cultivars of common couch (hybrids) in order to find the perfect turf. One promising one is Greenleaf Park, a cultivar selected for its vigour, low growth habit and colour. It is a dark blue-green colour, semi-dwarf so it doesn't need much mowing, and has so far demonstrated great hardiness under stress conditions. Of all the couches, it has also shown the greatest shade tolerance. It is denser than its parent couch. However, the one drawback is that it *must* be fertilised regularly. South African couch grass (*C. transvaalensis*) is said to be stronger wearing than common couch. Queensland blue couch (*Digitaria didactyla*) is better avoided in a children's lawn because it is the chief culprit causing grass stains on clothing. Its only advantage over other couches is that it tends to resist weeds better and forms a dense mat.

Carpet Grass (*Axonopus affinis*) This will grow well under trees, tolerating some shade, and is said to be a good hard-wearing, narrow-leaved carpet grass. Very versatile, standing a lot of hard wear, it is sold as seed by most garden centres.

Bent Grass The bent grasses make the lovely fine lawns you see on golf greens. However, both colonial bent or brown top as it is usually called (*Agrostis tenuis*) and creeping bent (*A. palustris*) are so vividly green and tender and lush that they are suitable only for luxury lawns and must be strictly avoided if children are to use them. Beautiful though they are, they simply will not tolerate rough foot traffic, nor are they any use in hot dry summers unless attention is positively lavished on them.

Kentucky Blue Grass (*Poa pratensis*) This is a good grass for cool and cold areas as it remains green all year, though it never gives that smooth shaven appearance of a really good couch lawn. It is a beautiful deep green colour and is the most resistant to wear of all the cool season grasses. It also tolerates dry spells quite well and is an excellent resister of frost. However, it will not tolerate low mowing and must be kept at about 5 cm height, giving a rather shaggy appearance as it tends to flop over.

Chewings Fescue (*Festuca rubra*) This is a cool season grass normally used for shade purposes, which remains evergreen during winter. It is not a good lawn for children, being a poor wearer like most of the shade-tolerant grasses. In a garden used by children, it is best to abandon attempts to grow grass in really shady spots and opt for tanbark or an ivy ground cover. Better still, use the shady area for a sandpit or a trampoline, which will prevent the children getting sunburned while they play.

Kikuyu Grass (*Pennisetum clandestinum*) Many people these days are looking at kikuyu as a backyard lawn because it keeps its green colour all year, makes a thick turf, is a really fast vigorous grower and will tolerate some shade. However, the broad leaves do not have that invitingly velvety pile that the couches offer and it is so extremely fast growing in summer that it can become a positive nuisance, requiring constant mowing to keep it at a nice carpety level (for it is not a dwarf grass) and invading borders, gardens and drains with its vigorous and aggressive growth habit. It is used on ovals and other places where extremely rough usage has to be tolerated, however, so if you need a football field down the back — and have the room — this is possibly the grass for you. Especially suited to warm temperate and sub-tropical areas.

Artificial Grass This is not a bad modern substitute for grass. Though it sounds a bit plastic, artificial grass can look quite attractive on home unit patios, in small courtyards, around swimming pools or in other relatively small areas. It can also be used in conjunction with real grass for those spots where the real grass won't take, such as under trees. Readily available from most garden suppliers.

How to help a lawn survive children

Once you've planted the right grass, here are a few ground rules that will help your lawn look as good as it can under the circumstances.

Rotate the position of hard-wear areas like swings, hammocks, cricket pitches and sandpits so that the worn bits get a chance to re-grow before the roots are totally destroyed.

Repair all badly-worn hollows (such as under swings, etc.) by sodding rather than by seeding. This not only fills in the hole, but is more likely to survive any premature traffic.

Work with the children's seasons rather than the horticultural seasons and you will come closer to success. For example, it would be foolish to re-seed the lawn just as the Christmas holidays commence. Fitting in with the games season is important too. Cordon off the bare patch under the netball hoop *after* the netball season, i.e. in summer when it won't be used for months. Re-sod the worn track down to the pool immediately winter commences, even if that's not the ideal time horticulturally.

When lawns get worn in a track, don't try to get children to take another route — it's doomed to failure. Instead, place stepping stones in the line of wear, making sure the stepping stones allow for a shorter stride than adults'. There are lots of quite cheap types of stepping stone available these days: cross-sections of logs look especially attractive. It might be a good idea to lay stepping stones along all well-used tracks in the garden, e.g. from back door to dog kennel, from back door to trampoline.

Lawns where children play suffer from compaction. Aerate occasionally to avoid excessive compaction by poking in the tines of a garden fork and gently loosening soil.

The stronger and healthier the lawn, the more wear it will take. Don't let the lawn get stressed enough

Lawns have to be tough

to become thin. Put on the sprinkler once a week in summer for a good deep watering, preferably in the evening so the lawn has a chance to drain before being trampled (many gardening books will tell you that this encourages mildew, but it's a matter of deciding on the lesser evil). Fertilise at least once a year (in spring) with a good lawn fertiliser bought at your garden store. Occasionally leave the catcher off the mower to return some nutriment to the soil via the cuttings.

Mow sensibly. Domestic lawns, to feel velvety as well as to be tough wearing, should be kept between about 50 to 100 mm in height and mowed regularly — once a week in the growing season, once a month in winter. The idea is to keep an even growth like a haircut. The worst regime is to let the lawn get long, shave it short, let it get long, shave it short. This weakens grass, particularly grass that gets heavy traffic. In fact, grass should never be cut very short.

Bear in mind that older children actually like mowing with hand mowers and hand mowers cut a good even lawn with much less damage to the grass itself. If you not only want to save yourself work but want to cut down on noise pollution and air pollution, buy yourself a hand mower.

Remember that children find mowing-day fun. They love the smell of cut grass. They love jumping in a pile of fresh lawn clippings.

4 Plants Kids Like to Eat

The trick with backyard crops is to grow the food your child actually likes to eat. It's no use producing kilos of chokos and radishes if the child loathes them. Nor are children, generally speaking, keen on exotic and unusual foods. The odd kid or two may adore artichokes — in which case the gardener's way is clear — but by and large, children like familiar ordinary vegetables and not too many at that! Fortunately, there are one or two easy-to-grow foods that children universally love from the home garden and this chapter has been restricted to those. Of course, if the rest of the family are keen vegetable eaters, the child gets a great education watching food being planted, watered, cropped, picked, cooked and then eaten, and seeing all those wonderful different shapes take form: broccoli, cauliflowers, lettuce. Children also love being sent down to the vegetable patch to pick stuff: some mint for the mint sauce, a lemon or a few leaves of spinach. But for actual eating — stick with the ones mentioned.

Another point. Don't expect children to maintain the vegetable plot in neat rows looking shipshape and weed-free, even if you've given them a separate little plot of their own. After a

'My vegetable garden'

'Me working in my vegetable garden'

burst of initial enthusiasm planting seeds, kids generally leave the vegies to look after themselves until enthusiasm is revived by discovery of a ripe crop.

Scrupulous housekeeping is the rule in growing vegetables for children. Nothing turns a child off its food so effectively as a cooked caterpillar nestling among the vegetables on its plate.

Vegetables

Fresh Parsley (*Petroselinum crispum*) Unlike adults, who use parsley mostly as a garnish or a flavouring, children eat parsley by the handful straight from the garden. This is excellent as parsley is a good source of vitamins and iron. Parsley is one of the most flexible of herbs and it will grow just about all year round in most climates in Australia. Best to grow it from seedlings, however, as it is a bit slow to germinate — but that's easy as parsley is almost universally available from garden stores in punnets. It will also grow easily in pots so is good for children who live in home units. It is said that an infusion of parsley is useful for fading

freckles which might be an idea for older children to try.

Carrots (*Daucus carota*) Children pull carrots from the garden while young and sweet and eat them dirt and all. They are best grown in a sandy soil, but almost any Australian soil will produce them. The old wives' tale is that they make you see in the dark and make your hair curl — and perhaps it is given some credence by their wealth of vitamins. Even if you don't usually grow vegetables, a row of carrots fronted by a row of parsley makes a fresh green border in the flower garden. Packets of carrot seed are available everywhere; choosing the seed can be half the fun as carrots come in lots of varieties and shapes — stumpy, baby, short, long and thin, round. At a pinch, even a deep pot will produce a couple of carrots.

Undersized, forked... but home-grown

French Beans (*Phaseolus vulgaris*) Unlike adults, who generally eat their French beans cooked, children love picking raw beans and eating them straight off the bush, which is great as far as their vitamin rating is concerned. French beans are one of the easiest plants to germinate from seed. Just push in the big seed and within a week out pops the plant. You can choose to grow beans Jack-in-the-Beanstalk-style as a climbing plant, or you can select the dwarf French beans which grow on a bush; it simply depends on which packet you choose. The beans themselves are practically identical. Try growing one on cotton wool on a saucer in the kitchen simultaneously so the kids can see what is happening underground. The only caution with beans is to supervise the picking, which can become so over-enthusiastic that the whole plant is wrenched from the ground.

Sweet Corn (*Zea mays saccharata*) Sweet corn is one of the outstanding backyard success stories. Not only is backyard corn much sweeter and milkier than shop-bought corn (so good that some kids eat it for breakfast), but it is one of the most dramatic vegetables to grow with its straight tall stalk, waving plumes, glossy silk and fat, pale green ears. Sweet corn is a summer crop and easy to grow from seed. Packets are available from all garden stores. Corn is a greedy feeder so buy a small bag of manure at the same time as you buy the packet of seed and dump them all in together. A special variety (*Z. m. everta*) can be grown for popcorn. Harvested when fully mature, this is a great treat. The grains of this variety are very high in starch; when heated, the moisture expands and they explode into the familiar popcorn.

Peas (*Pisum sativum*) If nothing else, growing a few pea plants will show children that peas don't self-generate, already packed in plastic and absurdly green in the freezer section of the supermarket. Kids love eating peas raw, straight off the vine, and indeed there's something immensely satisfying about opening up a pod and seeing a neat little row of peas lined up inside. Peas are now found in all varieties — mini peas, sugar peas, snow peas, as well as several more ordinary varieties. A winter crop, peas are planted from seed and are quite slow growing.

Radishes (*Raphanus sativus*) These have been included because they are so extremely fast-growing that they have become almost children's classics: plant the seeds on Monday, you'll see the first green leaves cracking open the soil surface by Thursday. However, though radishes are a beautiful red colour, and a nice satisfying round shape, I've yet to meet the child who has eaten more than the first radish off the rank. They generally find them a little too hot on the tongue.

Fruits

Strawberries (*Fragaria chiloensis*) Children love being sent out to pick strawberries. Searching for the red gleam of a ripe one hidden under the leaves makes the whole thing a game. Despite their luxury reputation, strawberries are surprisingly easy to grow. Plant them in any climate — tropical to heavy frost — and they will flourish virtually pest free except for the birds and the snails. Once you've got a couple of strawberry plants you're set forever because after fruiting they send out runners which make more strawberry plants. Before long, the children can give plants to their friends. If you want to grow them in the traditional way, get hold of a bale of straw and tuck it around the plants so the berries are kept off the ground by the straw … it looks very professional.

Children love to eat a pod of fresh peas raw

The fun of finding a hidden strawberry

41

Passionfruit (*Passiflora edulis*) Australian children take a passionfruit to school for lunch break — they just bite out a piece of skin and suck the juicy stream of seeds straight into their mouths. In the garden, passionfruit vines make decorative covers for a fence, a shed or a trellis — anywhere which is warm and sunny and sheltered. In fact they are almost worth growing for their exotically attractive flowers alone. Fruiting life is five to seven years only, but in this time they can produce enough passionfruit to fill many bowls with pure pulp. Easy to grow, it is best to plant a named variety from a reputable garden store. They also need some trellising for support. Passionfruit can be grown in a wide range of climates.

Oranges (*Citrus sinensis*) Orange trees do beautifully in all the middle range climates in Australia and are a good backyard crop because they are not subject to the scourge of the ubiquitous fruit fly like so many fruit. Even a small tree, given the right spot, warmth, plenty of water and a handful of citrus food now and again, will produce orange juice and cut oranges for most of winter — and you couldn't give your children fresher vitamin C than that. Oranges will bear (on grafted trees) after only two years, but a stronger tree is produced if the tree is not allowed to bear until it is four to five years old. Consult a reputable garden centre for the best variety for your area.

Pineapple (*Ananas comosus*) This tropical fruit grows well in home gardens up north or can even be tried as a pot specimen in a warm spot in the sub-tropics. If you plant a top cut off a bought pineapple in early autumn it will produce a pineapple the following summer. Pineapple cut up with mint is a good cool summer dessert, but better still, children like using the pulled-out leaves from the top of the pineapple as fingernails.

Unusual Backyard Crops

Peanuts (*Arachis hypogaea*) Planted the minute the cold weather is over, peanuts can make an interesting crop as a backyard experiment further south than you would ever have imagined. For seed, simply buy some fresh raw peanuts from your local health food store and plant them in a warm sunny spot. Peanuts have a curious growing habit. They are small clover-like plants which bear a pretty set of small yellow flowers in about 6 to 8 weeks. These are infertile. Then a set of fertile, hardly noticeable, flowers appears. From these flowers, long shoot-like peduncles or 'pegs' reach out and downwards, burying themselves in the soil. At the tip of each one of these, underground, a new peanut will grow. By late summer, when foliage begins to yellow, the peanuts are ready. Dig carefully with a fork and hang vines in a well-ventilated spot to cure for a couple of weeks. Peanuts are extremely nutritious, but are not recommended for children under five years because they can lodge in their lungs.

A different home crop: peanuts

The seeds of the cheerful sunflower are good to eat

Sunflowers (*Helianthus annuus*) These giant flowers, stretching tall, their faces following the sun in its daily path across the sky, are worth growing simply because they look like a child's drawing of the sun. They also happen to produce highly nutritious seeds that are great for children as nibbles. To produce edible seeds, just let the sunflowers stay in the garden all summer until the back of the sunflower head is brown and dry. Sunflowers will flourish almost anywhere hot, needing full sun all day. Unfortunately, birds love them too.

Baby New Potatoes (*Solanum tuberosum*) Feeling round in the earth for a possible crop of firm little baby potatoes is so exciting it is worth giving over a corner to this rather slow growing vegetable just so the children can experience that moment. No need to buy seed potatoes. Just find an old potato down the bottom of the vegetable basket, cut it into pieces so that there is at least one eye to a piece and shove the pieces in the ground. After many months, during which the potato bush will have flourished, flowered and the flowers died, you can begin thinking of digging. The little white potatoes — sometimes up to 40 per plant — are hidden in the soil among the roots of the plant. Even washing the dirt off your own potatoes is fun.

Mung Beans, Alfalfa, Bean Sprouts All you need for these indoor crops is water and a glass jar. Children in home units and flats can grow their own salads on the kitchen bench — and

The salad vegetable children can grow in the kitchen — mung beans

remarkably, all children seem to love eating handfuls of these fresh crunchy little baby vegetables either alone, mixed in sandwiches or with other salad vegetables. Given water and warmth, seeds germinate in a matter of hours and are ready for eating (in summer at least) in three days. Seeds are available in brightly coloured packets from most garden stores with full instructions printed on the back, but after you've seen how to do it it is usually cheaper to buy seeds in bulk from health food stores. Very high in vitamin content and a great TV snack.

Mini Vegetables Tiny vegetables are all the rage in the garden stores at the moment: mini beetroots, mini capsicums, mini cabbage, mini cauliflower, mini eggplant and many others. Two that might appeal to children are:

Mini tomatoes: These can be grown two ways — on dwarf bushes suitable for pots, or on specially developed normal-sized bushes which produce up to 500 mini tomatoes per bush in bunches like grapes. The big problem with tomatoes is fruit fly, but early planting helps as the worst of the fruit fly occurs after Christmas. Both types of bushes produce full little marble-sized tomatoes which burst satisfactorily in the mouth and can be used on children's salad plates in all sorts of imaginative ways — as eyes, nose, balloon, etc.

Mini watermelons: Watermelons are a classic favourite of children, but these are one better: grapefruit-sized and with just enough for two serves in them. Unlike regular water melons, they will grow in cool climates and the skin turns yellow when ripe rather than dark green. Inside, the luscious red flesh is just the same as regular watermelons.

Some Curiosities for the Vegetable Garden

Vegetable Spaghetti (*Cucurbita pepo*). Money might not grow on trees, but spaghetti can certainly grow on a bush. Just boil the ripe yellow gourds of this marrow-family plant whole for thirty minutes, split them open, scoop out the long strands of spaghetti and serve with bolognaise sauce and cheese. Served hot for dinner, it is almost impossible to tell the difference from pasta — but vegetable spaghetti is lower in calories. A quick-growing summer vegetable that will produce at least half a dozen marrows per plant. Marrows can be stored for up to two months. Available readily in seed packets from garden centres.

Serpent Cucumber (*Cucumis melo flexuosus*) Another amazing sight for the vegetable garden … a cucurbit that produces edible cucumbers that grow up to one and a half metres in length, coiling round and round themselves like a basket of snakes. Although cucumber does not have much food value, most children like the crunchiness of a few sticks with a salad.

Yard-long Beans (*Vigna sesquipedalis*) One bean would be enough for a child's dinner. These beans grow over a metre long! A pole variety originally from South-East Asia, this is a climbing annual, very easily grown from seed. It is related to the mung bean and also to the snail plant *Phaseolus caracalla.* Wonderful grown on a trellis with the long dangling beans hanging down waiting for the pot. A warm season crop. Stringless. Ready to eat six weeks from sowing.

Found foods are fun. Here it's honeysuckle but it could just as easily be a grass stalk

5 Over 50 Plants with Quaint Names

For thousands of years, gardeners have given affectionate names to plants they commonly see around them. Some are based on adult jokes that would not interest children, such as Mother-in-Law's Tongue, Bachelor's Buttons, Poor Man's Orchid, Woman's Tongue Tree and Lawyer Vine. But there are plenty more with names that appeal to children.

Some are plants that look so ridiculously like animals, humans, fish or household objects that the names are a perfect fit. Some are plants with such catchy nicknames they appeal to a child's imagination. Others have names that refer to some weird habit of growth with uncanny accuracy.

In this chapter, you will find a selection you might like to try in your garden. They are all suitable for Australian gardens, they are all decorative in their own right, yet they add that intriguing extra dimension that transforms an ordinary garden into a special garden full of surprise, interest and humour.

Moses in a Basket (*Rhoeo spathacea*) At first glance, people tend to dismiss this small purple-toned semi-succulent as a rather dull and gloomy looking plant. But lifting up one of the strap-like

Moses in a Basket. See the 'baby' asleep in its purple cradle

leaves immediately reveals the hidden flower that looks exactly like a tiny baby asleep in a miniature purple cradle ... a wonderful garden secret that all small children find irresistible. Moses in a Basket is an easily grown rockery plant equally at home in a shady spot outdoors or in a pot inside. It likes shade and grows in most Australian climates.

Just like lambs' ears

Lambs' Ears *(Stachys lanata)* Children love this furry plant ... and it's easy to see why once you take one of its soft felty wool-covered leaves between your finger and thumb. Each leaf feels just as you would imagine a soft little lamb's ear would feel. Lambs' Ear is a hardy little rockery plant and very easy to grow. Best of all, it produces its leaves at just the right height for children to enjoy — about 20 cm. A good reliable perennial, spreading densely to give ground cover. It thrives in seaside gardens and almost everywhere except the very hottest districts of Australia.

Starfish Flower *(Stapelia orbea asterias)* For children that love fossicking around in rock pools, this extraordinary succulent produces a flower that looks and feels exactly like a starfish — yet in their own backyard. An easy-to-grow rockery plant, it thrives in either full sun or half

The Starfish Flower

shade. Also known as Carrion Flower because the flowers have an extraordinary odour of rotting meat to attract blowfly pollinators. Likes warmth, but could be grown on windowsills in colder districts. Readily available in seed packets, but a bit tricky to germinate.

Baby's Tears *(Helxine soleirolli).* Children are always enchanted by the evocative name of this tender, bright green, tiny-leaved ground cover that can be scooped up by the spoonful and transplanted to make a new plant. It is suitable for damp places in almost any district except hot dry climates (in some places, it actually grows under water at the edge of clear streams). A very fast growing and attractive plant, it is so' low to the ground it almost looks like a vivid green carpet. It can be used as a softener for straight edges and even makes a pretty indoor plant in a low pot for a child's room, provided it has plenty of light and someone remembers to give it plenty of water.

The tiniest tenderest leaves of all: Baby's Tears

Painted Daisy *(Chrysanthemum carinatum* and *C. coccineum)* Rings of bright primary colour in broad brush strokes make the faces of these daisies look just as if they have been painted by the kindergarten class. A really bright flower that grows anywhere in full sun, but with a rather unpleasant smell. A summer-flowering perennial.

Fish Bone Fern *(Nephrolepis cordifolia)* Children run their fingers and thumbs down the spines of these hardy ferns and strip off the 'bones' of the fish's skeleton. Fortunately you can't kill them; they grow like weeds almost universally, especially in the shade and in old gardens.

Snapped next to the giant zucchini for the family photo album

Hear the clack of the castanets? The elegant Spanish Shawl (page 55)

School prawns swim through a gate (page 51)

Do you like butter? (page 61)

Making daisy chains (page 61)

Fishbone fern makes good feathers for an Indian headdress

Fronds are also useful as feathers for Indian head-dresses, wands, tucked in a belt for a grass skirt. Just dig out a portion of an established clump and plant.

Forget-me-not (*Myosotis alpestris*) The combination of the low soft shape, the prettiness of the tiny flowers, the quaint name, its easiness to pick and the fact that it is rarely considered precious by adults make this a perennial children's favourite. Prolific seeders, Forget-me-nots look gorgeous drifting under trees, and positively spectacular if massed in a bed — like a blue cloud hugging the ground. Best in cooler areas. Plants flower for about ten weeks in spring. Easily obtainable and even more easily grown.

Forget-me-nots

Grub Fern (*Polypodium formofanum*) Grow this in a hanging basket and watch bright green caterpillars squirm in and out of the sphagnum moss. The grubs are not real grubs, of course — they are the fleshy bright green snaky rhizomes of this hardy fern which, apart from anything else, is worth growing for its delicate green foliage alone. Available from any specialist fern grower and easy to grow provided it is kept well-watered.

Snail Plant (*Medicago scutellata*) This is a leguminous fodder plant from Europe known as Snail Medick because its coiled seed pods suggest snail shells. It has become naturalised in parts of Victoria and should be available from fodder and agricultural seed suppliers. Best grown in a pot or a rockery as a curiosity as its ornamental value is not high, apart from the startling seed pod.

Snail Flower (*Phaseolus caracalla*) Each strangely shaped flower is light purple to yellow, coiled backwards like a snail shell and about 3 cm across. Flowers grow in big sweetly smelling clusters on a twining evergreen creeper with a light bushy habit. Summer flowering. Thrives in temperate climates. Very easy to grow with flowers that last well when cut. Makes a good cover for stumps and fences.

Old Man's Beard (*Clematis aristata*) When the springtime blanket of pretty star-shaped flowers of this creeper die millions of white threads attached to the seedpods cover the whole vine like a thick soft fluffy old man's beard. It is very unusual and visible metres away. Grows anywhere sheltered, but likes woodland conditions of dappled light and moist leaf-mould soil best. It loves scrambling over nearby trees and shrubs, taking their shape, but not harming them. Grows in all climates.

Dutchman's Pipe (*Aristolochia durior*) The flowers of this vine look just like the fat thick-bowled tobacco pipes you picture Dutch burghers smoking by the canal-side — an amazing sight in full bloom in late summer and fun for children to pretend to smoke. It needs a frost-free position and a tolerant gardener who will let it run riot. Dark green glossy leaves. Good for places where other vines will not grow. Evergreen.

Black-eyed Susan (*Thunbergia alata*) A good name that sticks in children's minds. The bright orange flowers with their jet black eyes positively shout for attention in a woodland setting. Likes either full sun or dappled shade, but the more sun the denser the leaves and the more prolific the flowers. An open-growing evergreen climber that grows well in a wide range of climates. Considered a pest to urban bushland in Sydney.

Black-eyed Susan winks boldly from the bushes

Black Boy

Black Boys (*Xanthorrhoea australis*) It is remarkable that more Australian gardeners don't use this weird and unusual plant as a lawn specimen — a group of *Xanthorrhoeas* in a grassy glade with their stiff grass 'skirts' bouncing and 'spears' held high looks just like a party of black boys going hunting. Children would love to play among them. They are excruciatingly slow growers so it is essential that mature species are obtained. needs full sun, little water, no care and will grow anywhere.

Cup and Saucer Vine (*Cobea scandens*) A doll's tea-party table can be set by using the green and purple flowers of this rampant vine as crockery. Each flower looks exactly like an exquisitely shaped miniature cup balanced on its own saucer. Grown frequently in Sydney, but sometimes hard to get started. However, its alternate name — Mile-a-minute — should be heeded! Dies down in winter. Flowers in summer. Flowers last two or three days when cut.

The fly on the leaf is actually the calyx of the *Ochna atropurpurea*

House Fly or Mickey Mouse Plant (*Ochna atropurpurea*) The red flies with bulgy black eyes that cover this bush are not actually the flowers, but the red calyx and black seeds which follow the short-lived yellow flowers. Some children see them as Mickey Mouses with black ears. An angular shrub, 2 metres x 2 metres, the ochna seems to survive no matter how hot and dry the conditions. It is also considered one of the worst pests invading urban bushland because it is so difficult to remove.

Toothbrush Bush (*Grevillea longifolia*) In spring, this unusual shrub sprouts dozens of fat pink toothbrushes, so real-looking you feel you could clean your teeth with them. A really hardy Australian native for Sydney gardens, buzzing with bees and tiny honey-sucking birds at flowering time and spreading into a lovely shaped shrub, not tall. Likes good drainage and sun. Suits most climates.

The Toothbrush Plant

Drumsticks ready for picking

Drumsticks (*Isopogon latifolius*) The hard round seeds of this small native Australian bush look as if they should be rat-tat-tatting at a stretched skin, but unfortunately they don't come equipped with the long straight stems required. Not often grown in home gardens, but quite a neat little shrub of a suitable height for children to enjoy the drumsticks. Needs good drainage. Will grow just about anywhere.

Shrimp Bush (*Drejerella guttata* [syn. *Beloperone guttata*]) Large pink cooked prawns swim all over this bush when it flowers. The cooler the conditions, the brighter the colour of the prawns. Actually the segmented crustacean appearance is not formed by the petals but by the coloured overlapping bracts that practically conceal the flowers. 1m high. Full sun or slight shade. Capable of withstanding drought conditions. Very hardy. Colour plate page 47.

Bottlebrush (*Callistemon* species) Australians are so used to this plant they no longer register

Washing up with a bottlebrush

just how precisely like bottlebrushes the flowers are, but for washing-up games they are an essential item. Many species are now available, ranging in colour from white to hot pink to deepest red. In spring, the shrub can be literally dripping with rosellas and honey-eaters attracted to the heavy flush of blooms. So many hybrids are now available that there's a bottlebrush to suit every garden requirement.

Feather Flower (*Calothamnus quadrificus*) The dense red one-sided flowers of this very lovely dark-green Australian bush can be put to all sorts of uses by children for dressing up — they look extraordinarily like feathers. A very good garden plant whose leaves look almost misty from a distance, it grows everywhere except in extreme cold. To about 1.5 metres.

Feather flowers are useful for dress-up games

Caterpillar Plant (*Scorpiurus vermiculata*) Another leguminous fodder plant like the snail flower, this hardy annual is originally from Asia Minor. It is the seed pods that give it its name: they look so remarkably like caterpillars they are marketed in England in three varieties: plain, striped or hairy. May be difficult to locate, but worth asking agricultural seed merchants.

Staghorn (*Platycerium superbum*) Giant green antlers leap from the head of these bizarre-looking ferns. Another variety is the Elkhorn (*P. bifurcatum*) with similar antlers. Both grow attached to trees, brick walls, fences, patio walls. In the shade and kept moist, they will look after themselves for years. An added attraction for children is the white furry fuzz that covers the new leaves on which children love to 'write' with a finger, revealing the shiny pale green beneath. Very hardy. Needs a frost-free climate.

Red Hot Pokers: the name no child ever forgets

Red Hot Poker (*Kniphofia uvaria*) The plant with the name no child ever forgets. The red hot yellow and orange pokers are in fact dense spikes of lily-like flowers about a metre tall. The strap-like leaves tend to get a bit scruffy looking, so it is best planted down the back against a background of trees to glow hotly from a distance. Suitable for any district, any position, except extremes. Easy to grow ... and as bird attractors, can't be beaten. Eastern spinebills and wattle birds flock to them.

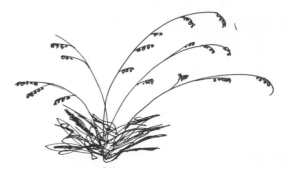

Angel's Fishing Rods

Angel's Fishing Rod (*Dierama pulcherrima*) Every five year old will want one of these. A South African bulb putting out incredibly delicate stems up to 1.5 metres long with dainty pink bells. Also known as Fairy Bells, Wand Flower, Fairy Wand and Fairy Fishing Flower. A small perennial for the cooler zones, liking a moist well drained position with full sun. May be a little difficult to obtain but well worth the effort. The 'wands' spring from a clump of mid-green grass-like leaves.

Bird's Nest Fern (*Asplenium nidus*) It is easy to imagine a family of birds taking one look at this fern and settling down in it to raise a family. The flat blade-like fronds form a perfect nest cushioned at the bottom with a soft pad of leaf mould. This Australian native can be grown in a pot indoors in which case it stays quite small, but planted out under the trees it can eventually grow into a nest big enough to house a peacock. Thrives in just about all climates.

Bird's Nest Fern

Pick the one that looks most like a kangaroo's paw

Kangaroo paw (*Anigozanthos* species) The strange and woolly flower spikes of this very Australian plant look a bit like kangaroo paws but it is worth planting for patriotic reasons alone as one of our more bizarre plants. A low plant with strap-like leaves, it thrusts up the flowers on long strong stalks 1.5 metres high. The red and green variety from Western Australia (*A. manglesii*) is the most beautiful, but the most temperamental. However, the green one (*A. flavidus*) grows magnificently on the east coast given good drainage and full sun.

Looking Glass Plant (*Coprosma repens*) This shrub is not covered in tiny mirrors, but has bright green glossy leaves so shiny they *almost* reflect your face. A brilliant plant for places where nothing else will grow, *Coprosma* stands high winds, salt spray, pure sand, total neglect. Best of all, the ultra-shiny leaves make excellent harmonicas if you hold two together and blow. Given time, *Coprosma* makes quite a good gnarled climbing shape. A highly adaptable plant.

Handkerchief Tree (*Davidia involucrata*) In sunlight, it looks as if there are white handkerchiefs hung to dry all over this tree. By moonlight, it looks as if a flock of doves has just alighted on the tree, giving it its other nickname, Dove Tree. A pretty addition to any garden, it will grow in any frost-free area, is deciduous and can reach 10 metres, though it rarely attains such a height. The white parts are actually bracts, not flowers.

Shaving Brush Tree (*Bombax ellipticum*) You could almost believe shaving brushes grew on trees after seeing this amazing plant during its flowering time in November. The shaving brush flowers stand erect, well separated and open one after the other all through November. A fast-growing sub-tropical tree with a very light timber not unlike balsa wood, it is best grown in the warmer parts of Australia only.

Flower of Shaving Brush Tree

Octopus Tree (*Schefflera actinophylla*) Less trouble than an aquarium. Plant an octopus tree in the garden and you will soon be producing huge red tentacled 'octopi' complete with

Press together two shiny leaves and blow for a great bush harmonica (*Coprosma repens*)

A red octopus against a blue sky

'suckers'. Almost unkillable. Sometimes called Umbrella Tree, the leaves are used by children as toy umbrellas. Although this tree is often used as an indoor plant, it will reach 12 metres in height with a sturdy trunk if you let it romp away in the garden. Just chop it back if you want it to produce octopi at child's eye level. Grows readily almost everywhere.

Elephant's Foot Tree (*Beaucarnea recurvata*) An extraordinary plant from the deserts of Mexico. The bulbous lower trunk of this tree swells out and stamps on the ground exactly like an elephant's foot, the wrinkled grey bark adding to the illusion. Doubly strange, it is also known as the Pony Tail Tree because each branch ends in a dense clump of grass-like foliage that trails down for a couple of metres. Much used as an indoor plant, *Beaucarnea* will grow to a 10 metre tree if planted out in ordinary garden soil. Best in dry warm gardens.

Very like an elephant's trunk

Elephant's Trunk (*Agave attenuata*) This remarkable rosette-shaped succulent sits there looking quietly decorative in the rockery most of the year until suddenly it puts forth the most astonishing inflorescence — a huge curving elephant's trunk, 4 metres long, rounded and covered with tiny white flowers. Quite a sight. This is one of the safe agaves with no spines. Unlike most succulent rockery plants, it prefers a position slightly shaded from the strongest sun, but it will grow in very poor soils.

Elephant's Ear Tree (*Enterolobium timbouva*) The elephant seems to have been some sort of professional model when the plant world was being conceived. This small tree has large leaves resembling an elephant's ear. Plant an *Enterolobium* near the Elephant's Foot Tree (above) and the Elephant's Trunk Plant (above) for a pachyderm corner. There is even an Elephant's Ear Lily (*Colocasia esculenta*) that could be planted underneath. *Enterolobium* is a very ornamental tree with racemes of white flowers in spring.

Doll's Eyes (*Harpullia pendula*) Don't look now but you're being watched. The seed pods of this tree are the reason for the name. They grow in joined pairs like a dumbbell. As the pods mature and brown, they split slightly so that the black 'eyeball' or seed squints through the lowered 'eyelids' exactly like the doll's eyes that are inserted into doll's heads. Also known as the Tulipwood Tree, this pretty weeping tree with its bright green foliage grows to about 3 metres and is native to Australia's east coast, so it will grow well in just about any garden.

Which are the real doll's eyes?

Tennis Ball Tree (*Agathis macrophylla*) One of the very tall southern hemisphere conifers, this Pacific Island kauri is slow growing and a bit too big for the average home garden, but a tree covered in tennis balls might be difficult to resist if you have a tennis court. The pale tennis balls are actually the cones but look amazingly realistic. An example can be seen in the Royal Botanic Gardens in Sydney.

Goldfish Plant (*Nematanthus wettsteinii*) Although many people call the *Columneas*

Anyone for tennis?

Amazingly like goldfish ... the flowers of the *Nematanthus*

Goldfish Plants, they are beaten hands down by the *Nematanthus*. Each curious pouched flower of the *Nematanthus* with its constricted mouth looks exactly like a goldfish swimming through the leaves, especially as the colour is a golden orange-red. To make the illusion more complete, if you put one in a glass of water and squeeze, it blows a bubble. A plant that requires good humidity and a warm spot, *Nematanthus* can be grown outdoors in Queensland but needs a warm indoor spot in New South Wales. Very polished small bright green leaves and semi-trailing habit make it an ideal plant for hanging baskets.

Spanish Shawl (*Heterocentron elegans*) This embroidered-looking ground cover from Central Mexico drapes over garden edges looking like a carelessly-flung Spanish shawl, its flamboyant magenta flowers glowing like sateen against a closely-stitched fabric of tiny green leaves. Very quick-growing effective ground cover for warm temperate climates. Colour plate page 47.

Bird of Paradise (*Strelitzia reginae*) The extraordinary resemblance to a bird's head and the unusual combination of colours — orange with a tongue of unexpected deep blue — compensate in children's eyes for the rather hostile appearance of this stiff fleshy large plant with grey-green erect leaves that grows so well in hot exposed conditions. A good indestructible plant.

This Bird of Paradise (*Strelitzia*) stares cheekily at the camera

Tassel Fern (*Lycopodium phlegmana*) Granny's curtains seem to have been the model for this Victorian-looking fern which provides a bit of old-world lushness, especially for those who remember playing hide'n'seek in the parlour's velvet drapes and tassels. A lovely fernery plant, it needs warmth, shelter and moisture.

Like the tassels on Granny's velvet curtains

55

String of Beads

String of Beads (*Senecio rowleyanus* or *citriformis*)
This dainty hanging-basket plant with long threads of pale green balls is often called Baby's Bottles or Hanging Footballs, but to me the name String of Beads is best, because it looks most like a display of jade necklaces. An easily grown succulent suitable for indoors and ferneries.

Prayer Plant (*Maranta leuconeura*) An extraordinary little plant. All day long the leaves are held at right angles to the stem. As night falls, they start to move, slowly but visibly, until they are pointing up, lying close to the stem and suggesting an attitude of prayer. By the child's bedtime, they are praying. A wonderful present in a pot for a child, it grows well indoors — in fact, it must not be grown in full sun. Only about 30 cm high. As an extra bonus, markings on the leaves look a bit like rabbits' tracks.

Telegraph Plant (*Desmodium motorium* or *gyrans*)
In warm sunlight the unusual leaflets of this little indoor plant jerk up and down like a signalling semaphorist, hence its name. Some people think the plant looks as if it is fanning itself. Either way, it is quite comical to see a plant acting like a human being. *Desmodium* will grow outdoors in Queensland but in New South Wales would have to be called a hot-house plant, though it could possibly survive the winter on a warm windowsill in the bathroom or kitchen as long as it is kept moist. Quite an enchanting novelty with violet flowers.

Hen and Chicken Daisy (*Cladanthus arabicus*)
This amazing daisy practically turns into a blossom quilt. First each individual daisy flower bears three or four more daisies around its perimeter — hence the name hen and chicken. Each of these blooms then forms three or four daisies round *its* perimeter. Each of these blooms then does the same thing and so it goes on until there is a spread of two feet or more of blossom, all attached to each other. Rather difficult to get seed of this plant. Suitable for use in rockeries. Pleasantly scented. Bright yellow flowers. About a metre in height, forming a pretty mound of pale green foliage and flowers.

Living Stones (*Lithops* species) These peculiar but tiny succulents (2 cm x 2 cm) are widely marketed in pots by garden centres; a quick glance could easily mistake them for a couple of

The Prayer Plant will fold its leaves at bedtime

Living Stones — six tiny cacti in a pot

little pebbles which is, in fact, their alternative name: Pebble Plant. A native of South Africa, they are a lovable oddity very suitable for a child's sunny windowsill or the rockery. One amusing variety is called Split Granite (*Pleiospilos bolusii*) and looks like a small piece of polished pink and black flecked granite with a cut engraved across the top. *Lithops optica* is also interesting: it is called the Window Plant because the succulent leaves are almost entirely buried in soil, except for a little translucent window on the upper surface which filters light down to the delicate green underground parts.

Bottle Tree (*Adansonia gregoryi*) This grotesque tree whose swollen trunk looks so exactly like a grey bottle does actually store water in the hollow chambers of its light fleshy wood. Another variety of Bottle Tree (*Brachychiton rupestre*) grows such a hugely swollen trunk that in former times they were hollowed out and used as lock-ups or storage sheds. *Adansonia* is a medium-sized, drought-resistant tree suitable for both arid-climate and temperate gardens.

Blowfly Grass (*Briza maxima*) This is one of the plants found in the pockets of urban wasteland so frequented by children — adults consider it a weed and would never actually plant it. It is, however, quite an attractive grass with its big segmented seed heads dancing in the wind and looks quite attractive in among cut flowers.

Walking Palm (*Pandanus odoratissimus*) This amusing tree looks as if it is about to walk into the sea on its stiff aerial roots when grown in a seaside garden, especially as the onshore winds tend to tip it slightly backwards. Actually the main root and the lower stem decay, leaving the stiff aerial roots springing straight from the stem, heightening the illusion of legs. Suitable for warm coastal gardens, the pandanus is a tall shrub or small tree.

Three Pandanus going for a walk

Blowflies

Nature's pop art: the bottle tree

More Plants with Droll Nicknames

There are so many comical, apt, intriguing names in the plant world the list could go on and on. Here are just a few extra ones that come to mind from my childhood … I'm sure your family has plenty more special favourites of their own to add.

Maidenhair (*Adiantum capillis-veneri*)
Curly Wig (*Caustis flexuosa*)
Egg and Bacon (*Dillwynia retorta*)
Spider Flower (*Cleome spinosa*)
Yesterday, Today and Tomorrow (*Brunfelsia calycina*)
Granny's Bonnet (*Aquilegia vulgaris*)
Poor Man's Weatherglass (*Anagallis arvensis*)
Running Postman (*Kennedia prostrata*)
Fred Flintstone's Gourds (*Cucurbia pepo*)
Propeller Plant (*Crassula falcata*)

Fairy Hair or Curly Wig: an Australian native rush

Propeller plant: the aerodynamic succulent

Yesterday, Today and Tomorrow. Yesterdays are purple, todays are mauve, tomorrows are white. Or is it the other way round?

6 Plants to *Do* Things With

Only adult gardeners spend time standing back and admiring the subtle spring colour combinations of the azalea bed. Plants that you can *do* something with attract children. Children not only have an amazing knowledge of the 'useful' plants in their neighbourhood, they also have a very idiosyncratic interpretation of 'useful'. Did you know, for example, that the chief attraction of an agapanthus is its fat bud, which you whip off with a stick? Did you know that clivea leaves are mashed up to make a juicy 'soup'? Or that you snap off the long slender leaf buds of ginger plants and have a competition to see who can unfurl them fastest without tearing the tender young leaf? Fortunately, these destructive tendencies can be curbed if you explain that a particular plant is a treasure and *must* be respected, not only in the home garden but in the neighbour's place too.

This chapter describes some favourite plants used for a variety of purposes by Australian children. They are all easily grown in the backyard. Among them you will find some weeds, some old garden favourites, some surprise uses and a few novelties that will interest even adult gardeners to grow and use for themselves.

Urban wasteland: the city child's delight and the gardener's salvation. Wild fennel to crush and smell. Dandelion flowers to flick and dandelion seedheads to blow the time on. Convolvulus flowers to suck against your nose and mouth. Lantana flower heads to pull off and throw

Plants Commonly Used by Kids

Duck Plant (*Sutherlandia fruitescens*) Children love to float the shining pale green inflated seed pods of this small shrub in a bowl of water where they look exactly like a flock of ducks paddling round. A bowl of them would make a wonderful centrepiece for a children's party. An erect-growing, soft-wooded small shrub growing up to 2 metres in height, *Sutherlandia* does best in a fairly dry sunny spot and produces hundreds of 'ducks' in late summer.

Float a swan in a bowl of water

Swan Plant (*Asclepias fruiticosa*) Much the same shape as *Sutherlandia* seed pods (above), the inflated silvery-green seed pods of this little shrub have tiny 'feathers' on them so that when floated on a bowl of water they look more like amusing little fledgling baby swans than ducks. *Asclepias* is doubly interesting to children because it also hosts the caterpillars of the beautiful Monarch Butterfly. A fairly quick-growing but short-lived shrub, it is easy to grow again from the seeds it produces. Suitable for most districts. A native of South Africa. Grows to about 2 metres.

Iceland Poppy (*Papaver nudicaule*) Children watch until a little split of colour appears in the round poppy bud, when they know the twin furry caps can be gently prised back to allow a dramatic tumble of bright crumpled petals to emerge — quite an astonishing amount to be packed into one small bud. Children also use poppy flowers for making 'poppy babies', curving back the petals and tying a sash round the waist with a blade of grass. The black centre of the poppy forms the head, the long stalk the legs. All in all, with its tall slender leafless stem holding high its bright coloured cup flower the poppy is one of children's favourites, especially as they bloom in winter when fewer flowers are out. Easily obtainable everywhere as seeds or seedlings.

Snapdragons (*Antirrhinum majus*) Very young children enjoy playing dragons with the velvety jaws of these bright old-fashioned flowers, snapping them shut over their fingers. The flowers grow on lovely thick spikes half a metre in height and are very hardy. They are available in a selection of bright colours and are planted as annuals from seed or seedlings.

The snapping jaws of an old favourite — the snapdragon

Busy Lizzie (*Impatiens wallerana*) At a touch, the ripe seed pods of this pretty shade-loving plant burst open with a violent elastic snap. Because of this, Busy Lizzie is one of childhood's favourite plants, widely grown in many Australian gardens and obligingly producing thousands of seed pods so there is almost always one ready to pop. A perennial about half a metre tall, producing masses of attractive single pink, white and red flowers year round. Grows easily from a cutting poked in the ground. Does well under trees and in moist areas. Not suitable for tropics.

D.G.

The spring-loaded seedpod of the Busy Lizzie

Buttercup (*Ranunculus repens*) If you hold one of these flowers under a person's chin (so the legend goes) you can tell whether or not they like butter (colour plate, page 48). The glossy lacquered yellow petals make a shiny reflection on their skin if they do like butter. Often found naturalised under trees or along the sides of laneways, this old-fashioned plant from England is easy to grow, very pretty, but needs lots of water and spreads so easily it is considered a pest to urban bushland.

Dandelion (*Taraxacum officinale*) No need to actually plant dandelions. The gardener normally sees his job as getting rid of them. Nevertheless, being weeds and therefore not considered precious, several parts of the plant are used by children. The fluffy seed heads are used to tell the time by blowing. A harmless

What's the time, Mr Wolf? One o'clock? Two o'clock?

weapon can be made by tying the stalk in a knot and flicking the dandelion head off the top by jerking the knot. Occasionally the long-stalked flowers are used for making daisy chains. As an extra bonus, the leaves can be used in salads.

Daisy (*Chrysanthemum maximum*, the Shasta Daisy, or *Aster novi-belgii*, the Michaelmas Daisy) Daisy chains are part of everyone's childhood (colour plate p. 48) and everyone remembers pulling off daisy petals one by one, chanting 'he loves me, he loves me not' or 'tinker, tailor, soldier, sailor'. Fortunately they grow easily from cuttings — in fact, they are probably one of the easiest and showiest plants to fill a garden with. Earmark the ones you like from gardens in the neighbourhood, then slip out after dark and take a cutting. If you push it into the ground and water it, in no time you will have a daisy bush. Daisies can be pink, white, yellow or blue and grow almost anywhere.

He loves me. He loves me not. He loves me....

Moss (*Bryophyta* species) If you are lucky enough to have a damp spot with some moss growing there naturally, don't scrape it away, children love it. They use moss for lining little nooks to make fairy houses, as a background for flower pictures, to line budgerigar graves, as carpets for doll's houses. Though moss gardens are common in Japan, moss is not usually sold in Australian garden shops, nor are people generally familiar with different types of moss.

Trigger Plant (*Stylidium* species) These very dramatic flowers are much sought-after by the children who know them. The flower has a unique device for pollinating its species. It holds its pistil and stamens full of pollen ready cocked and waiting. When the plant is touched (by bee or child) the trigger releases with an astoundingly strong elastic snap. Half the fun is searching for a trigger that has not yet been activated. These little native perennials have basal grass-like leaves and flowers that can be white, cream, yellow, pink or red but are most often pink, arranged in a loose spike. They bloom in late spring and summer. Easily available from native plant nurseries.

Agave (*Agave* species) To carve their initials on the smooth fleshy leaves of the agave plant is a temptation few children can resist. The letters soon brown to a satisfying permanence leaving a personal signature in the garden. The only problem with agaves is that the leaves end in wicked spikes, so don't plant them where children might accidentally fall on them. Agaves prefer a hot, dry, totally neglected situation, but will grow almost anywhere.

Banana Palms (*Musa* species) Bananas have several attractions for children apart from their obvious eating qualities. The stiff purple bracts that enclose the banana inflorescence are shaped like miniature rowing boats and make great racing craft to send down swollen gutters. The big flat leaves make wonderful picnic plates. The curious cellular trunks are so easily penetrated with a sharp stick they act almost like fibreboard. Though best grown in the tropics, bananas will often give good crops further south provided a warm spot and water is provided. As long as they are protected from the birds while ripening, they have few diseases.

Cotoneaster (*Cotoneaster lacteus*) Red cotoneaster berries, produced in their millions by even small bushes, are a prized ingredient in backyard 'soup' when stirred together with a handful of leaves, a dollop of water from the hose and a sprinkle of dirt. Other uses are for throwing by the handful, as marbles, as trail markers, as dolls' eyes, as pattern makers. Cotoneasters are not suitable for the tropics and are sometimes considered a pest to urban bushland.

Veronica (*Hebe speciosa*) Children pinch open one of the slim closely-folded leaf buds of this

A great place to carve your initials, but watch out for the spikes

The leaf bud of the veronica pulls open to reveal a smaller leaf bud which pulls open to reveal a smaller leaf bud which pulls open....

compact evergreen New Zealand native shrub to find that inside there is another closely folded leaf bud which they then pinch open to find yet another closely folded leaf bud… It's a bit like playing with a set of those Russian dolls that fit inside one another. A smooth-leaved hardy little shrub with purplish sprays of flowers in spring, suitable for temperate and cooler areas.

Bamboo (*Phyllostachys aurea*) One of the most useful plants in children's eyes. Given a pocket knife and a clump of bamboo, children can manufacture bamboo flutes, bows and arrows, tapping sticks, fishing rods, rafts, ceremonial archways… the list is endless. Bamboo makes a wonderful living green wall to screen off part of the garden too, though its roots are very invasive. There is also a black-stemmed strain (*P. nigra*) available which is extremely decorative. A very hardy plant but not, unfortunately, loved by neighbours. Grows anywhere. Needs no care. Best grown, I think, in a concrete pot which confines the roots.

Mountain devils look out for marauding children

Mountain Devil (*Lambertia formosa*) School holidays on the Blue Mountains would not be complete without a packet of pipe cleaners and a walk to collect the green and brown seed pods of this prickly bush. In front of the fire, you then twist two or three pipe cleaners together to make a body, add the horned seed pod as a head, make a tail and a pitchfork and *voilà* — a mountain devil. A bit prickly as a bush, but nice and compact with showy red flowers in winter. Grows almost anywhere except the tropics but needs perfect drainage.

Honolulu Lily (*Solandra guttata*) This rampant vine produces huge fat flower buds in summer which are full of liquid that can be squirted if you squeeze the right place. Buds that survive turn into huge trumpet flowers that can be blown as toy trumpets, so the plant is a double winner.

Bamboo is one of the most useful plants to children, used for bamboo flutes, bows and arrows, tapping sticks, fishing rods and a million other important artefacts.

Great squirt bombs: the buds of the Honolulu lily

63

Unfortunately it is one of those vines that tries to follow its owner to work in the mornings, but is an excellent heavy cover plant for fences, neighbour privacy or noise reduction. Throws out unusually long cane-like branches. Grows extremely rapidly in Sydney given warmth and water, but best in tropical or sub-tropical zones, being frost-tender. Also called Cup of Gold Vine.

Hibiscus: one of the flowers children like to 'undress'

Hibiscus (*Hibiscus rosa-sinensis*) Big brightly-coloured flowers that children 'undress' are the attraction of this spectacular, widely-grown shrub of the tropical and sub-tropical areas of Australia ... they pull off the sepals first, then the petals, then the pistil ... The many different varieties and colours of hibiscus, its long flowering period and its fast-growing nature make this a wonderful small evergreen shrub for children's gardens: best of all, any flowers they pick will be replaced by the plant the next day. It produces literally hundreds a year.

Walking Grass (*Bromus diandrus*) Seeds that 'walk' up the inside of your sleeve are the remarkable attraction of this grass to children. A raspy rough seed ear has minute little bristles that cling to fabric. As you move around, a seed that has been inserted at the wrist emerges at the neck. A trick beloved of small boys.

Raspy grass heads that 'walk' up your sleeve

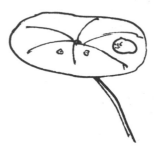

A drop of water on a nasturtium leaf can be rolled around like silver mercury

Nasturtiums (*Tropaeolum majus*) The best thing about nasturtiums is the water-resistant leaves. A drop of water on a flat round green nasturtium leaf rolls round like a beautiful silver 'diamond, never wetting the leaf. Nasturtiums are great for picking too, so bright with their orange, yellow and red flowers and so prolific that in summer they are constantly in bloom. A trailing annual, nasturtiums are easily raised from seed and are so hardy they are almost a weed. The young leaves can be used in salads.

Bush music

Children make bush music from many plants. Eucalyptus leaf harmonicas. Coprosma leaf whistles. Bamboo flutes. Tapping sticks from pieces of wood. Drums from a stick on a hollow log. Blades of long grass twanging. Seeds in a dry gourd. A rustling bunch of dried leaves.

Smells that stick in your mind forever

The smells of childhood gardens provide each of us with our personal nostalgia. New mown grass. Crushed ants. Wild dill and fennel crushed between your hands. Lemon grass. Coconut geranium. All the herbs, expecially mint. The smell of *Cestrum nocturnum* on a still summer evening. Violets. The Christmas smell of gardenias. The wonderful combination of earth and rain before a storm. The extraordinary banksia that smells like hot urine.

Cherry earrings (page 69)

Popping fuchsia buds (page 70)

Illawarra Flame Tree (page 71)

Wind fishing (page 74)

Garden kitsch is lovely! (page 78)

...but it depends on personal taste

...and varies from the twee   ...to the arty

Copenhagen ceramics elegantly scattered on a lawn

Have Fun with these Oddities

A famous gardener once said, 'Queerness, when it is extremely queer, is attractive to children.' Here are some plants that are rarely grown in Australian gardens but which are in fact easily available and would certainly be enjoyed by children if they had them. All are very odd, interesting and unusual.

Sensitive Plant (*Mimosa pudica*) One of the most entertaining plants ever. Whenever you touch it, the whole plant actually recoils. The feathery leaflets quickly fold together, the leaf stalk droops and the whole plant gives the impression it is cringing. Recovery is quite rapid. In fact, the reaction is an adaptation to prevent drying out — in wind, the whole plant seems to pack itself away. A very decorative little annual, only about 20 cm high, with attractive feathery foliage and pink puffball flowers. It is now available quite readily from nurseries. Response is most rapid at temperatures of 25° to 30°C, but it fails to respond at temperatures below 15°C. Can be grown on a pot on a warm windowsill in cooler districts, though it probably won't survive a winter. Outdoors in the warmer parts of Australia it spreads rapidly.

The sensitive plant shuts down its leaves so rapidly they blur for the camera

Obedient Plant (*Physostegia virginiana*) This amusing plant recalls those rubber-covered wire figures with arms and legs that bend into position that children were playing with a few years ago. Children push the flowers that emerge from the square stalks of this plant into different positions around the stem — and the flower remains in the position to which it has been pushed. Because of this, it also has the name of Docile Plant. A native of North America, this pretty perennial with rose-pink flowers like snapdragons is very hardy, about 24 cm tall and flowers in autumn. Flowers are brightest in semi-shade. Available from specialist seed merchants.

Gas Plant (*Dictamnus alba*) On a hot still day, you can put a match to this incredible plant just near the base of its very pretty inflorescence and whoosh — it flares up momentarily, igniting the lemon-peel scented gas that the plant emits but leaving the plant itself uninjured. Sometimes called the Burning Bush, this little perennial is best grown in a dry place which stimulates production of oil by the glandular stem. The volatile and flammable oil is lemon-scented. Indian fire worshippers regard this plant as sacred. Rather difficult to obtain in Australia, but easily propagated from seed if you can locate some in overseas seed suppliers' catalogues. Allow this trick only under supervision.

Vegetable Sponge (*Luffa aegyptica*) No need to go diving in the Aegean to get your next bathroom sponge when you can grow one of these sponge plants in your own backyard. Just pick the mature fruit, cut off the ends, extract the seeds and leave in a dry place. The flesh will wither, leaving the familiar network of fibre which may be used as a bath sponge. Seeds may be difficult to germinate unless you soak for twenty-four hours before planting. To promote fruiting, pinch out trailer tips when trailers reach 150 cm.

Walking Stick Cabbage (*Brassica oleracea longata*) A remarkable variety of cabbage from the Channel Islands. Instead of forming a low

Walking stick cabbage

round head close to the ground and producing the familiar vegetable called cabbage, this plant shoots up a two metre stalk, straight as a broomstick and interestingly segmented, which in the Channel Islands is cut, dried and polished to form a splendid walking stick. In Australia, if you plant in early spring, the walking stick should be ready in time to make a Christmas present for grandpa. Quite readily available in seed packets from garden centres.

Carnivorous Plants Plants that shut their jaws and trap a living fly present such a deviation from normal plant behaviour that they are endlessly fascinating to children. A stall at Paddy's markets that sells these things is more crowded with children than the pet section on Saturday mornings. The variety is enormous in carnivorous plants and with care and a bit of knowledge of their habits (for example, they like wet feet) you can have quite a collecting of snapping, gobbling, weird-looking creatures. Start with the Venus Fly-trap (*Dionaea muscipula*) whose vicious jaws can be tricked into believing a fly has landed by simply touching them. Then there's the curiously etiolated *Sarracenia flava* into whose long tube the insect walks further and further in search of sweet food, only to find itself trapped by the plant's hairs and the lid of the tube. Most of these survive happily in pots for years.

Soap Pod Tree (*Acacia concinna*) Just rub the naturally-lathering pods of this small tree straight onto wet hair and you have the ultimate in natural shampoos — non-irritating, giving the silkiest, most manageable hair ... and cheap. A native of tropical Asia, this leguminous thorny tree also produces sour leaves which are used as a substitute for tamarind. Frost sensitive, suitable for warmer parts of Australia only. A real novelty, but seed may be difficult to obtain.

Cotton (*Gossypium hirsutum*) Looking rather like a small hibiscus, the attraction of the cotton plant lies less in its flowers, pretty as they are, than in the fat pure white cotton balls that burst out all over the bush in late summer, wrapping the seeds in a flurry of fluffy cotton balls. Fascinating for children to see the raw material of their school shirts and socks growing in the backyard — and unusual as a dried arrangement indoors. If you have a long hot growing season and access to plenty of water, try some, but keep it dry at harvesting time.

More Plants Children Find Useful

Cherries	A pair of ripe cherries as earrings (colour plate page 65)
Roses	Put a pulled-off thorn on your nose and pretend to be a rhinoceros
Gladioli leaves	Weaving mats. The leaves of other bulbs can be used also, providing they are flexible

Weaving mats from bulb leaves

Pineapple leaves	Fingernails
Thistles	Gossamer seeds sometimes called Father Christmases. So light they bowl across water without getting wet.
Umbrella trees	Leaves used as umbrellas
Angophora trees	Rubbing the nodules out of the dimples in the smooth trunks
Kennedia vine	Listening to the seed-pods make an audible pop in a friendly way during the night

Banksias	Grey nodules on big bad banksia men seed pods are rubbed off to show the rich brown velvet beneath
Convolvulus	Floppy pale blue flowers are sucked over the mouth and nose
Fern fronds	Uncurling them
Agapanthus buds	Whipping them off with a stick

Unfurling fern fronds is so *satisfying*

Whipping the buds off the agapanthus

Grass clippings	Mixing them with water to make stink bombs
Autumn leaves	Finding one of each different colour — yellow, gold, scarlet, purple, pink, orange, brown, rose, copper
Mistletoe	Giving someone a kiss under it

Sticky weed	Making patterns on your jeans or playing 'sticky witch' with it
Ginger plant	Unfurling the new leaf spears
Privet hedges	Bouncing off
Fuchsia	Popping the buds (colour plate page 65)
Honesty	Rubbing off outside skin of seed capsule
Conifers	Decorating at Christmas
Lantana	Flower wars
Sticks	Peeling and whittling

Sticky weed is better than fuzzy-felt for making patterns on your track suit

Hedges are good for bouncing off

Lantana is normally considered a weed by adults so pulling off the flowers for a flower war is OK

Kids can decorate this conifer for Christmas

Kids love to peel or whittle sticks, then rub them against sandstone rocks to make them warm

7 Planting for the Imagination

Gardens are such a potent force in children's lives. Probably no other place where children spend their time witnesses such imaginative play, such extravagant make-believe. Remember the stories told by big sisters and brothers of bunyips lurking down the back of the garden? Or how scary the creaking branches of the big tree were at night? To a child, the garden can be a fantastical, romantic, legendary place, peopled with imaginary characters, wild woods, fairies, cowboys and Indians. Mostly, children can be left to take care of this side of things very adequately without adult help, but if you are interested in the fanciful side of children's natures, here are some plants and ideas that will make your garden just that little bit more original and special...

Plant a red tree. Confirming all those finger paintings children do in kindergarten where the faces are green, the sea is yellow and the clouds are purple. The amazing flame tree (*Brachychiton acerifolium*) is *red!* It looks that way at least, when everything else is green. Quite a spectacular sight even for an adult, in full bloom it looks almost luminous. The flame tree is a native of Queensland and New South Wales, a hardy tree, growing to about 12 to 18 metres under cultivation. The seed pods, which are shaped like rowing boats, are much used by children as gutter craft. The only drawback is

Like a child's picture book illustration — a totally red tree — the Illawarra Flame

that the tree takes about seven years to bloom and even then is an erratic flowerer. In a good year, however, it is unsurpassed. Bird attractive. Best in a sunny position which is sheltered from the wind. For enhanced colour fantasy, plant near a jacaranda.

Have a pink tea-party on this drift of blue carpet

Plant a blue tree. Ever since a book called *Sally in Rhodesia,* which I was given as a child, described a pink afternoon tea served outside under a flowering jacaranda tree with the mauve blooms above and a carpet of fallen mauve blossoms below, I have coveted a jacaranda tree *(Jacaranda mimosifolia).* Driving through Sydney's suburbs in November, these blue trees in full bloom make a patchwork quilt of the landscape, dappling the green with a blue so intense, so unique, it is almost impossible to record with a camera. Like the flame tree, its special attraction is that the tree flowers before it puts out its new spring leaves, so the tree is for a few weeks entirely blue. Will grow in a wide range of climates but get a good sized one in first place or it might take years to bloom. An added attraction for children is that you can blow the fallen blooms up like bubble gum until they pop.

Plant a row of flower faces. Apparently the pansy *(Viola x wittrockiana)* looks up with such a gentle wistful expression on its velvety flower face that it appeals to almost all children. The similarity

The wistful little face of the pansy

The shock of a black flower

to a face is not so striking to an adult (for a start, adults are not low enough to look a pansy straight in the eye), but nevertheless pansies are a decorative annual for a border and come in wonderful shades of yellow, purple and blue. There's even a startling black pansy being marketed now. Pansies are very easy to grow as seeds or as a punnet of seedlings from your local garden centre. Flowers appear in spring and summer. Children use pansy flowers to make faces for 'paper dolls' on the lawn.

Four-leafed clovers. Looking for a four-leafed clover *(Trifolium repens)* for luck is one of the traditional pastimes of Australian children in summer. Fortunately there's no need to *plant* clover in the lawn. All too often it mysteriously appears; the problem is, rather, getting rid of it.

Puzzle picture: find the four-leafed clover.

D.G.

Fuchsia ballet dancers pirouetting on their points

Grow a corps de ballet. Every child calls fuchsias (*Fuchsia fulgens*) Ballet Dancers and twirls them round in a pirouette between finger and thumb, yet curiously this has never become the accepted popular name. They are also in much demand as doll's house lampshades. Despite their fragile weeping appearance, fuchsias are very hardy garden standbys, profuse flowerers (which is fortunate because children also like to *pop* the buds), and do well in almost any climate, though they need savage pruning in winter. These days there are an enormous number of reliable varieties to choose from. Among those whose flowers resemble ballet dancers most are 'Fiona' (flower is slender and long-torsoed with white arms flung out and skirt a pink bell), 'Spring Bells' (flower has a scarlet torso and a twirling fluffy white tutu), 'Caroline' (flower is all pink with a pink bell-shaped skirt and pink arms folded above the head), 'Prelude' and 'Winston Churchill' (they are both dressed in fluffy Zandra Rhodes outfits with layered skirts, one in pale pink and white, the other in pale mauve and pink).

Grow a pet in a pot. A miniature plant in a pot is far less trouble than a budgerigar or a puppy and just as loveable. It can even sleep beside the child on the bedside table. These days, miniature plants like cactus, ferns and palms in tiny pots are readily available in garden centres, placed shrewdly near the cash registers. They come in a wide variety of species (all the more fun for choosing), are extremely hardy and put up with a lot of neglect before they perish. Better still, they usually cost no more than about $2 — hardly a major outlay — and thrive on nothing more expensive than water.

Wilbur. A good substitute for a pet

73

A wishing tree by decree. If you have a free-standing tree with a substantial trunk and good access all around, you have all the necessary ingredients for a wishing tree. Just declare it a wishing tree — by tacking up a notice if you like — and you'll catch the interest of every child for blocks around. Years ago, every park worth its salt had one and children adored them. The idea is that you run three times round the tree (with or without your eyes closed, depending on local rules) and then silently make a wish. As long as you don't tell anyone what you wished, it's bound to come true.

Leave the fairy rings in the lawn. Although gardeners may view the appearance of this lawn fungus with horror, children have traditionally believed that the circles have been made by the feet of fairies dancing on the lawn overnight. The fungus spreads in circles, sometimes causing mushrooms to grow round the outside of the ring, sometimes causing a greener ring that stands out against the paler lawn colour.

A shower of postage stamps. Schizopetalon walkerii are said to be the only square flowers in existence, though a close look at this white flower of the mustard family from Chile shows that the four petals are merely arranged to give the impression of a rectangular shape. The postage stamp effect is achieved by the petals having fringes round the edges which look like serrated perforations. At twilight, a border of Schizopetalon is said to resemble nothing so much as a flutter of postage stamps dropped accidentally on the ground. A pretty border plant with slender branched stems to 20 cm, its flowers open at night and give out a scent of almonds and vanilla. Rather hard to come by, however.

Bells, wind chimes and other wind toys. Cheap, easy to hang on a branch, yet such an effective way of giving a sense of theatre to the garden. Bells and wind chimes come in all sorts of forms — glass, ceramics, shell, metal — and can be hung outside the child's window so they can be heard as he or she is going to sleep. Colourful fish wind-socks hung from the trees give an almost Japanese look to the garden. Colour plate page 65.

Mounds. Don't underestimate the attraction of a mound. Though comical in concept, commercial landscape gardeners have long realised their potential. For some reason, children love sitting on a mound. Cover one with grass and it provides the perfect slope for them to roll down. Cover one with sweet-smelling thyme for a perfume like the hills of Rome. One of the chief added attractions of a mound is that it is a cheap way of getting rid of a pile of excavated soil which otherwise might have to be carted away at great expense.

Bird baths and feeders. Anything that will attract birds to the garden gives the place an air of excitement. A bird bath helps. Feeding them helps too. At any pet shop you can usually get those seed bells for wild birds that you hang in trees. Many people make simple tray-like bird feeders into which they put a mixture of bread, honey and water. Planting some nectar-filled native plants like kangaroo paw attracts native birds. There are also plenty of bird houses marketed commercially and scaled to suit different sizes of bird which you can put in the trees to attract them. Children are very fond of pigeon-houses — the old fashioned cylindrical sort with serrated roof and a multitude of windows.

A stone stream. Next best thing to having a gurgling stream of water through your garden is a stone stream. This is a Japanese idea, in which cleverly collected and placed stones wind through a little slope of grass to *look* like a stream. Children love tricks of the eye like this.

Grow a vine curtain. Unusual garden treatments catch children's imagination. A vine curtain of clematis, jasmine, *Cissus antarctica* or honeysuckle could be used to screen off a child's cubby house, form a door to another part of the garden or just as a simple visual effect.

Plant a literature corner. This is a pretty ambitious

Passing children love this living garage door

concept which depends on the child's and the gardener's taste in literature, but a start could be made with one or more of the following suggestions:

Ferdinand's cork tree (probably *Quercus occidentalis*)

Andy Pandy's willow tree *(Salix babylonica)*

Snugglepot and Cuddlepie babies *(Eucalyptus purpurea)*

Big Bad Banksia Men *(Banksia serrata)*

The big bad banksia man glares balefully out from his prickly lair

Peter Rabbit's vegetable garden

Jack's beanstalk *(Phaseolus vulgaris)*

Hutu and Kawa's New Zealand tree *(Pohutukawa)*

or even an historical plant: the nardoo that kept Burke and Wills alive *(Marsilea* sp. plate page 83)

Plant a witch's garden. An enterprising nursery in Bowen Mountain, New South Wales, used to sell a magical mystical parcel of nineteen plants that have played an important part in witchcraft. In the collection there's *Angelica archangelica* and *Avens* used as amulets against evil, there's betony to protect against unwanted dreams, there's basil and cumin to use in love filtres, there's four-leafed clover. Instructions for witches were apparently included in the package. Unfortunately the nurserywoman seems to have flown off on her broomstick because simple mortal telephone calls have been unable to rouse her. Of course it is possible that she has merely cast a spell on herself and will soon wake up. In the meantime, you could plant a silver birch *(Betula pendula)*. The thin whippy twigs of this ancient European tree are said to be used by witches to make their broomsticks, while their

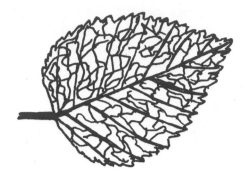

Leaf of the witch's favourite tree: the silver birch

gleaming silvery-white trunks and open habit give a sense of eerie remoteness to the garden. Only suitable for cooler areas, however.

Plant a giant flower. If you want to add a surrealistic look to your garden, this is how: plant a Gymea lily *(Doryanthes excelsa)* which throws up a gigantic bright red flower on a 5 metre high stalk. Quite extraordinary. This Australian native plant can be seen growing in startling naturalness on many New South Wales coastal highways, never failing to give the observant driver a shock of surprised disbelief. An easily grown, fast plant for large gardens, but not suitable for terrace dwellers or introverts. Another surrealistic plant is the giant fig, but you have to be lucky enough to own one already.

Living surrealism: the hanging roots of the giant fig make a fairytale grotto

Sausage tree

Grow a delicatessen shop. Imagine fat thick sausages hanging down from long strings beside a display of small cheeses. Sounds like a delicatessen shop but it's actually a garden. One of the world's most unusual trees, the sausage tree *(Kigelia pinnata* or *africana)* is a 16 metre tall member of the Bignonia family originally from the River Nile. It first puts out velvety red flowers, descending on 7 metre long stems from the topmost branches. After pollination by night-flying insects, the seed pods, which look like metre-long, thick-as-your-arm sausages, are produced on the end of long dangling strings. Though they *look* exactly like sausages, they are in fact hard and utterly tasteless to eat. This tree grows well in semi-tropical Australia, especially on the coast. There is one in Sydney's botanical gardens, and seeds are readily available from specialist seed suppliers. The cheeses are not nearly as spectacular as the sausages, but interesting. They are produced by the cheese tree *(Glochidion ferdinandi)* and the cheeses are in fact the small plump round yellow seed pods hanging down well clear of the leaves. However, even apart from the cheeses, this small rainforest tree with its shiny leaves is an attractive addition to the garden. Likes a warm sheltered spot with plenty of water.

On midsummer nights kids can stain themselves blue with woad

Plan a druid dance for Midsummer Eve. Plant some woad *(Isatis tinctoria)* and the children can stain themselves blue with the juice from the leaves like the ancient Britons. Just imagine them capering round a bonfire with the spooky shadows cast on the trees, their faces dyed and a witch's brew bubbling in the cauldron. Woad, unfortunately, is one of the few plants mentioned in this book that might be difficult to obtain, though it is easily raised from seed and grows well in most parts of Australia as long as it is kept moist. It produces small yellow flowers in early summer. A hardy biennial of the mustard family indigenous to Europe.

Planting carpets. After rain, a number of shrubs and trees make beautiful carpets on the grass with their fallen blossoms. Rhododendrons are one. Jacarandas of course. Poinciana trees in the tropics. Even a red bottlebrush makes a feathery sort of carpet while the petals of apple blossom trees after a storm can cover the whole garden with a light drift of snow. Soft sweet smelling carpets are produced by the fallen needles of pine trees and casuarinas. The lemon-scented gum produces a pungent lemony-smelling carpet.

Attempt to break a record. The Zucca Melon *(Lagenaria suceranna)* is a mighty melon-making machine that will produce melons so big that you, the children and IT may not fit in the backyard together. Melons over 45 kilograms are quite common, often nearly two metres in length. You might even make the Guinness book

of records. Other suitable uses would be for 'guess the weight of the melon' competitions at school fetes, as photographic props, humorous birthday gifts or giant Jack-o-Lanterns.

The weirdest plants of all — cacti. Children are invariably fascinated by the extraordinary cactus

Peanut cactus

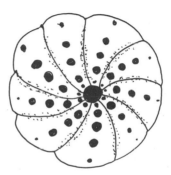

Sea urchin cactus

Bunny's ears cactus

family. Cacti are great for children's own gardens because they thrive on almost total neglect provided they are planted in a sunny dry well drained spot with cool rock-shaded soil for the roots. Try *Rebutia krainziana* which produces flowers twice the size of the plant itself. Or the

Rat-tail cactus

Old Man Cactus (*Cephalocereus senilis*), a hunched little individual covered in long wisps of grey hair. Or the tall thin columnar cactus which pops out brilliant perfect white flowers for one day only. There's even a 'rude' cactus pot being marketed by some garden stores lately. Cacti illustrated are Rat-tail Cactus (*Aporocactus flagelliformis*), Peanut Cactus (*Chamaecereus sylvestri*), Bunny's Ears Cactus (*Opuntia Microdasys*) and Sea Urchin Cactus (*Astrophytum asterias*).

Garden kitsch. Children love garden kitsch, but seem to make no distinction between the tasteless and the elegant. One family I know dotes on a crumbling cement stork that peers out of a tangled bed of asparagus fern, the iron reinforcing in his neck flaking rustily. There's a town in North Queensland that has turned into a sort of kitschland, with front gardens full of caterpillars made from old motor parts, old-tyre swans and polished winking hub cabs used as mosaics Mercifully, there are one or two almost passable examples of this genre available in fancy garden shops: little brass birds that fit over the handles of garden taps, or a charming crop of realistic little ceramic mushrooms. See colour plates on page 66.

Children Like Mothering Plants

An attendant who works in a big suburban garden centre makes the following interesting observation. Invariably, she says, children who are visiting the nursery with their parents appear at the counter possessively clutching the most bedraggled, neglected-looking plant in the place. To the parents' horror, the *only* plant that the child wants to buy is this bent, sad-looking object in a pot. Don't underestimate the helpless appeal of a neglected living thing.

A territorial gesture — this garden is *ours*

This garden is MINE! Two footprints marked firmly and permanently in concrete are a unique way for young children to leave their mark on the garden. Buy a bag of ready mixed cement from your local hardware store — all you have to do is just add water. Pour a small slab (or step) anywhere the children would like to mark as *their* place. When the concrete is nearly dry, have them carefully step in the cement.

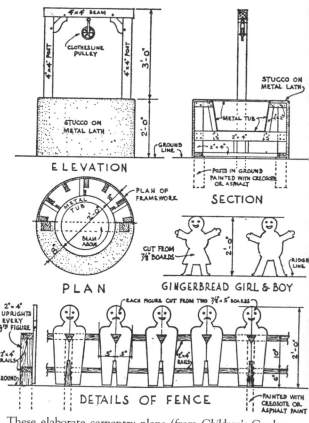

These elaborate carpentry plans (from *Children's Gardens*, Edwin L. Howard, 1950) show that adult gardeners of another era had more fun creating the garden than the children probably had playing in it

8 Twelve Garden Tricks

ere are twelve bits of foolery with plants that will amuse children almost as much as they will entertain the gardener. Eleven of them are quick, easy and cheap. Number 12 is extremely complicated and probably won't work anyway.

1 Grow a rainbow. A rainbow garden is one of the cheeriest sights you are ever likely to see. First, make a visit to your local garden centre and select seven punnets of annuals in the seven colours of the rainbow (see below). Then you simply rake flat a cleared garden bed, draw the outline of a rainbow on it with a stick and plant your annuals in colour bands like a rainbow. This is best done in spring because there is more flower variety available then, and it works best when plants are used instead of seeds because the flowers are more likely to come out simultaneously. The following suggestions have a bit of height difference between the colours, but there are probably plenty of combinations available in your garden centre that would ensure all bands of the rainbow are roughly the same height.

Red	Salvia (*Salvia splendens*)
Orange	Marigold (*Calendula officinalis*)
Yellow	Marigold (*Calendula officinalis*)
Green	Italian parsley, or mint
Blue	Ageratum (*Ageratum houstonianum*)
Indigo	Lobelia (*Lobelia erinus*)
Violet	Purple pansies (*Viola* x *wittrockiana*)

2 Radish writing. Children adore this trick. With a stick, print the child's name in big letters on an empty flat garden bed. Sprinkle a packet of radish seeds into the grooves and tamp down lightly. Within a week, the child's name will be written in little radish plants — BEN or SOPHIE or REBECCA. There are infinite

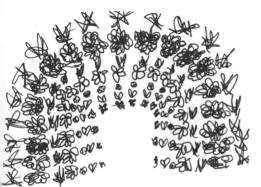

A rainbow garden in full bloom

variations on this. The radishes could pop up saying HI or HELLO. Or they could say HAPPY BIRTHDAY. Radish drawing extends the range. How about a Snoopy? Or a big smile? If you are really smart, you could use careful timing to give different changing images. See colour plates page 83.

3 *Fish into whales.* This is a summer project in the vegetable garden. Plant some zucchini plants — pumpkins or watermelons would also do though zucchinis crop more quickly. They all grow easily from a packet of seeds. When the zuccinis begin to crop, select a small zucchini about 12 centimetres long and, while it is still attached to the plant, carve the simple outline of a fish into the skin with a sharp knife. Leave the zucchini for about a fortnight (still growing on the zucchini bush) and then look again. The fish will have grown to a whale on a zucchini now 50 centimetres long.

Baby zucchinis ready for carving or bottling

4 *Marrow Magic.* This is a variation on the old ship-in-a-bottle illusion. First, plant some zucchini seeds in the vegetable garden and wait until they start cropping. When the first tiny zucchinis begin to form at the back of the flowers, select one and, while it is still attached to the bush, gently insert it through the neck of an empty bottle which you have washed in readiness for the moment. Take care not to snap the stalk of the zucchini. Rest the bottle gently on the ground with the zucchini still attached to the plant, taking care to tuck it well under the leaves to shade it from the sun. Check every day to observe progress because zucchinis grow fast, but in about a week the zucchini will have become so large you can cut the stalk and pour in

some pickling brine. Friends will be amazed at how the zucchini got into the bottle. It's a bit bizarre, but it uses up a lot of old bottles.

5 *Grass Ball.* This is a great way of recycling tired old bathroom sponges. Soak an old sponge thoroughly. Roll it in grass seed (mustard and cress would do too — anything thick and fast-growing). Hang it up in a sheltered spot under a tree … and hey presto, a grass ball. In some garden shops you can buy little porous ceramic animals that can grow a furry coat of grass on their backs using this same principle.

6 *Carrot Basket.* Plant a row of carrot seeds and let one of the plants grow into something pretty substantial. Pull it out. Cut the carrot off about 5 cm from the top, leaving all the green leaves on the stump. Hollow the stump out until it becomes a little bowl. Hang the thing upside down in the window and fill the little hollow with water. Soon the green fronds will curve gracefully upwards, forming a bizarre sort of self-generating hanging basket. Keep the water in the little bowl topped up, however.

7 *Fern Figures.* For patient gardeners only. You will need to start off with an established squirrel's foot (or hare's foot or rabbit's foot) fern growing in a hanging basket for this. Preferably use a basket without a full bark or moss lining so that the curious hairy rhizomes show. With a pair of pruning secateurs wielded judiciously, train the furry rhizomes into amusing animal shapes as they grow (see illustration).

The very prestigious and weighty horticultural reference book, A.B. Graf's *Exotica*, has a wonderful photo of *Davallia bullata mariesii* rhizomes trained as a monkey — that's Hare's Foot Fern or, more precisely, Squirrel's Foot Fern

The goose — a 13 year old's first attempt at topiary

8 *Home Topiary.* Create an elephant in your backyard, or a Snoopy, or a baby duckling, with the age-old art of topiary. Any fast-growing, thick, hedge-like plant will do to learn on. Simply take the hedge clippers and keep trimming as it grows until it takes on the shape you want, which is limited only by your imagination: perhaps a set of living tables and chairs, or a seal balancing a ball on its nose. If you live in a misty place, the sight of grey mist swirling round surrealistic topiary shapes creates a wonderful eerie effect. Suitable plants for the purpose are readily available. Cotoneasters are excellent, so are many of the cypresses. The small-leaved privet (*Ligustrum sinense*) is also excellent though considered a pest by many gardeners. In England they use box trees, which are a bit slow, but which are available here and look very attractive in a pot. All plants normally used as hedges are also suitable: *Lonicera nitida*, *Photinia glabra*, *Murraya paniculata*. One of the very best would be the gold-leaved olive (*Olea africana*) which is suited to most climates and withstands heat and drought extremely well. For the hot dry inland, the boobialla (*Myoporum montanum*) is a good quick grower and clips well.

Frame topiary is an alternative form of topiary. For this you simply train a thick fast-growing vine-like plant around and among a frame which has been fashioned to the shape you want. The variety is only limited by the skill of the frame-maker. Perhaps a giraffe? Or a giant cup and saucer? You can even use an old umbrella frame stuck in a pot and grow an umbrella. Many rampant climbers would do the trick. Two that come to mind are New Zealand Ivy (*Muehlenbeckia*) and *Cissus antarctica*.

9 *Fruit Shapes.* In Tudor days, when they loved things curious and fanciful, gardeners placed fruit in moulds while it was young and still hanging on the tree. As the fruit swelled and ripened, it was forced into the shape of the mould. You could have cucumbers shaped like a cross, apples in the shape of pears or lemons, any fruit at all in the form of men, beasts or birds. Using casting moulds available from craft or art supply shops, or experimenting with household shapes, you too could produce a weird Tudor fruit bowl, or, more mundanely, square tomatoes for the school sandwiches.

10 *Colour Magic.* This is not a trick that provides what you'd call an instant sensation, but it's an interesting long-term demonstration of man's power over nature nevertheless. The trick turns on the fact that hydrangea blooms are pink in lime soils, blue in soils where iron is present. By adding the appropriate substance you can turn the next year's flowers on your hydrangea bush to the opposite colour. Best to take a photograph of the previous season's blue flowers, however, or your powers as a garden magician who can turn flowers pink might be doubted, because memories are short. Aluminium sulphate will do instead of iron to produce the blue colour.

11 *Listen to a tree.* This fantastic idea was first suggested by Joseph Bharat Cornell in a wonderful little book called *Sharing Nature with Children* (Ananda Publications, 1979). He claims that if you press a stethoscope firmly against a tree you can hear the sap rising — the living heartbeat of the tree. The best time to do this, he says, is in early spring on a deciduous tree when the tree sends up its surges of sap after the long cold winter. I haven't tried it myself, partly because I have the greatest difficulty hearing even a human heart through a stethoscope, but apparently the most important rule is keeping the stethoscope completely motionless so there are no interfering noises. Good luck.

12 *Floral Clock*. This is the complicated trick. The idea is to plant blocks of flowers in sequence for each hour of the day and night — 1 to 24 — either in a traditional circle or a line. You will probably need a yard the size of a football field for this one, plus encyclopaedic horticultural knowledge, but no matter. You first clear a big open space, divide it into 24 segments and then plant in those segments the flowers that open at that hour of day. Theoretically, there *are* flowers that open at specific times of the day and night, for example, morning glory (convolvulus) is said to open at 4 a.m. and gazanias at 9 a.m.

The whole idea of a floral clock was apparently experimented with by the famous botanist Linnaeus. Though it sounds intriguing, if a little straggly, I regret to say I cannot vouch for the reliability of the clock, nor guarantee that the plants mentioned are obtainable. Nor have I been able to find plants to fill the two or three blank hours on the clock. In fact, if any readers have any suggestions, I would love them to let me know via my publisher.

For what it's worth, then, here are the suggestions for the floral clock, filched shamelessly from the lady who first suggested the idea (Sally Wright in an American publication called *Gardening: a New World for Children*). They have been adjusted neither to southern hemisphere time, daylight saving, time of year nor any other rigorous testing system. The only helpful suggestion I have to offer is that planting in full sun would make the clock more reliable.

4 a.m.	Dandelion. Morning Glory
5 a.m.	Poppy. Wild Morning Glory
6 a.m.	Cape Marigold (*Dimorphotheca*)
7 a.m.	African Marigold (*Tagetes*)
8 a.m.	Pinks. Pimpernel
9 a.m.	Portulaca. Gazania
10 a.m.	California Poppy. Golden Star of Texas (*Xanthisma texamum*)
11 a.m.	Star of Bethlehem
12 noon	Ice Plant
1 p.m.	—
2 p.m.	—
3 p.m.	Vesper Iris
4 p.m.	Four O'clocks. Marvel of Peru (*Mirabilis jalapa*)
5 p.m.	Jimson Weed
6 p.m.	Evening Primroses. Honeysuckle
7 p.m.	—
8 p.m.	Night-scented Stock. Datura
9 p.m.	Nicotiana. Moonflower (*Calonyction aculeatum*). *Cestrum nocturnum*
10 p.m.- Midnight	Night-blooming Cereus

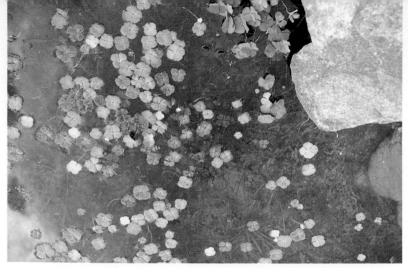

Plant a little history: the water plant nardoo whose seeds
kept Burke and Wills alive for weeks (page 75)

Days four and fourteen of the Grand Radish Writing
Experiment (page 79)

The waratah — a bit too stiff to be loveable

'Wilt thou marry me, my beloved?' (page 93)

9 Children Hate...

Plants are rarely neutral in children's eyes. Children have strongly held dislikes and can always point out the examples of hated plants in the district. Curiously, there is a surprising correspondence between the views of children of all ages and all areas on these matters: some plants are almost universally disliked. The following is a list of many of these, plus a few that are hated for more personal reasons. No doubt the children in your family have a few pet hates of their own.

Cutting Grass or Sword Grass This is far and away Australia's most hated children's plant. It includes many species, among them the native cutting grass (*Gahnia* species), pampas grass (*Cortaderia selloana*), lemon grass and others. The long strap-like leaves with razor-sharp edges inflict vicious little cuts to the hand. As an informant pointed out, you can't even pull it out because it cuts you worse. It is partly the false appearance of usability that makes this plant so annoying and frustrating. It *looks* as if it could be used for tying up the dog or tying up packages or weaving mats, yet one touch teaches better. It is also frequently located on a slope just where a child decides to pull himself up by grabbing a handful of it — to his sorrow.

The most-hated plant: cutting grass

Buffalo Grass (*Stenotaphrum secundatum*) Thoroughly disliked by almost every child. The dull grey-green colour and tough unyielding appearance of a buffalo lawn is the very opposite of the tender green sward on which children like to lie or do handstands. They dislike the prickly feel of the broad harsh leaves — which in fact often do produce a slight contact rash on tender young skin.

Bindii (*Saliva pterosperma*) Groans and shrieks are the universal response to the mention of the word bindii. These vicious little hooked-seed plants that lurk in Australian lawns are the scourge of children's feet all summer long.

Children are expert identifiers of bindii and can usually avoid walking on affected lawns. However, it is the frustration of seeing a perfectly good lawn ruined for bare feet that makes the bindii even more insufferable.

Stiff, Fleshy, Regimented-looking Flowers Gladioli, cannas, iris, tulips. These types of flowers are almost universally disliked by children. When you think about it, there is something cold and discipled about a tulip, despite its fine bold colours. It is not a loveable flower, standing stiffly in rigid uncompromising rows with the stalks making a leathery creaking sound.

On the subject of fleshy plants, many children dislike the common little succulent that grows so commonly on sandy banks: the pig-face. As it is neither disciplined nor regimented, and as it produces quantities of seemingly-pleasant brightly coloured flowers, I am not sure why it is so disliked.

Despite its bright flowers, many children have a strong dislike of pig-face

Dry, Hairy-leaved Plants Just why these plants are generally disliked is unclear. Perhaps it is the sensation of those leaves dryly rubbing against each other, making a sound just as nerve-jangling as the squeak of chalk on a blackboard, that is the problem. The small shrub *Lasiandra* (now called *Tibouchina*) is a case in point. Also salvia, and that very nasty plant with the furry flowers called Lion's Ears (*Leonotis leonurus*).

Dark Plants Plants with a generally dull purple look or plants in dark rusty red-browns are generally disliked by children. There is a particular one that is a favourite in old Sydney gardens (*Acalypha wilkesiana*) which has beefsteak-red leaves with paler edges. Children find these plants give a gloomy depressing look to the garden.

Banksia robur looks menacing

The dark and gloomy-looking canna

Some Personal Dislikes Found Among Children

1 'I hate gidgee — it smells revolting.' This was from a child in outback New South Wales; on checking it was *Acacia cambagei* she was talking about. At the approach of rain or when wet, the foliage emits a particularly offensive smell, so strong that it can be almost unbearable. It is native to the dry area of inland temperate Australia.

2 'I hate the tree that broke Emma's arm. Every time I pass it, I kick it.' This personalisation and anthropomorphising of plants is common.

3 'I hate full-blown roses.' This is an interesting and curiously mature hate, as the full-blown rose is in fact a frequent adult symbol of death, decay and the approach of winter.

10 What Not To Plant... Poisons, Irritants and Other Backyard Undesirables

There are so many plants in the world that are dangerous or poisonous to children to compile a comprehensive list would be an enormous task. For this chapter, I have confined myself to those plants most commonly planted in suburban and country gardens in Australia. I have concentrated especially on plants that are not generally recognised as being dangerous. If the list makes you feel like rushing out to the garden and pulling out half the plants, think twice before you do. Most of these plants have a very wide occurrence in many parts of Australia, yet very few children ever die. Simply being aware of the dangers is usually sufficient protection, though of course if you have a little baby at the crawl-and-put-it-in-your-mouth stage, you might have to take more positive steps. Poisons experts report that pesticides and weedicides are far more common causes of backyard poisoning than plants.

I have deliberately excluded discussion of plants whose pollen is said to cause respiratory allergies because there is so much contradictory and confusing information about it that it is not possible for a non-medical person to sort it out. To give one example, the acacias, long suspected of being prime culprits, are now less frequently thought to be responsible, as acacia pollen is so heavy it tends to drop to the ground beneath the shrub. These days, plants with lighter pollen grains, such as the grasses, are suspected of being the more likely cause of pollen allergies.

Be-still Tree (*Thevetia peruviana*) This beautiful shimmering small tree is commonly grown in gardens in warm areas of Australia, more often in Brisbane and other parts of Queensland than in New South Wales, yet it is lethal. The kernels and fruit are so poisonous that one seed is enough to kill a small child; even the milky sap and gorgeous golden trumpet flowers are extremely dangerous. Called 'dangerously beautiful' like many poisonous ornamentals, the Be-still Tree has a lovely open lacy appearance and its spidery foliage moves constantly in the slightest air movement. Usually 3 to 4 metres in height.

White Cedar (*Melia azedarach*) This very decorative flowering small tree, sometimes known as Cape Lilac, China Berry or Bead Tree, is found in gardens in almost every country on earth, yet the ripe fruits are highly poisonous to human beings. Children are reported to have died after eating six to eight ripe fruits. Widely planted in New South Wales, the tree has a spreading crown that provides splendid shade in summer, a spring flowering of loose sprays of lilac and purple flowers, followed by big clusters of berries, green at first but turning yellow as the summer proceeds. The clumps of berries persist after autumn leaf fall, giving the bare tree a most attractive winter aspect. Strangely, the fruit are poisonous to neither cattle nor birds. A very drought resistant and hardy tree. Grows up to 8 metres.

A dangerous and commonly grown ornamental: *Datura*

Angel's Trumpets (*Datura* species) These large (4 metres) soft-wooded shrubs with beautiful huge white trumpet-shaped flowers, heavily perfumed and produced in flushes throughout the hotter months of the year, are the source of drugs in several countries of the world. Natives of South America, three species are cultivated in Australia — *D. candida, D. suaveolens* and *D. sanguinea,* all of them poisonous. Many cases of human poisoning are on record, mostly children who have eaten seeds or fragments of flowers. Delirium and hallucinations are usually followed by complete recovery, however. Even rubbing the eye after touching the flower will produce dilation of the. pupil, due to the presence of belladonna in the plant. Widely grown in Sydney.

English Yew (*Taxus baccata*) An evergreen, short-trunked tree that grows excruciatingly slowly though extremely long-lived (in England there are probably still some yews from which Robin Hood could have made his longbow). All parts of the plant are toxic except, curiously, the red outer covering of the fruit, the poisonous principle being taxine, an alkaloid that depresses the action of the heart causing it to slow down and eventually stop. Poisoning, however, is usually due to deliberate ingestion of leaves or whole fruit. In Australia, the yew is a sombre, pyramid-shaped conifer with dense foliage.

Arum Lilies (*Zantedeschia aethiopica*) Fatal poisoning of children has been reported after eating the white spathe or yellow spadix of these commonly grown, beautiful and well-loved flowers. Symptoms are swelling of tongue and throat, acute gastritis, severe diarrhoea and death from exhaustion and shock. Arum lilies are found in many parts of Australia, usually growing in damp soil or shallow water, and the flowers bloom temptingly at child height (about 1 metre). Whether *Arum proboscideum* is also poisonous I have been unable to ascertain. This is a wonderful plant with a flower that looks like the posterior of a mouse bolting to cover with a defiantly waving tail.

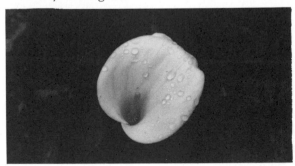

Arum lilies are poisonous — and dangerously tempting at child height

Castor Oil Plant (*Ricinus communis*) A conspicuous and attractive soft-wooded shrub with very large glossy palmate leaves. The castor oil plant is sometimes a robust annual, but more often a small tree to 3 metres, found naturalised in many parts of Australia, especially on creek banks, vacant lots, old gardens, neglected parts of parks and other places where children frequently play. A lethal dose can come from

Beware the deadly seeds of the castor oil plant

eating two to eight seeds; even more dangerously, symptoms do not usually appear straight away, but might take from hours to several days to develop (though eating the seeds does produce a burning in the mouth). In some cases there may be extreme sensitivity to a single seed due to allergic reaction. The fruit of the castor oil plant are very conspicuous, borne in clusters, each fruit being about 2 cm with or without soft prickles. The seeds are shiny and mottled.

Black Bean (*Castanospermum australe*) The Queensland Black Bean Tree is an Australian tree that many people believe poisonous … yet it is not quite as lethal as its reputation. It is true that eating the very large seeds of this big tree — either raw or roasted — does sometimes produce severe painful diarrhoea, but no deaths have ever been reported in children. It is possible that its reputation may have been made more lurid by reports of another tree known as Black Bean (*Erythrophleum chlorostachys*) which is extremely poisonous to stock. This tree, however, is not used as a garden ornamental. *Castanospermum australe* is a large handsome tree to 17 metres with dense dark compound foliage and orange and yellow pea flowers in spring and summer. It is a slow grower found only in frost-free areas.

Golden Chain Tree (*Laburnum* species) This beautiful small deciduous tree with its soft textured foliage, covered in early summer with hanging chains of yellow pea-like flowers, is extremely poisonous, especially in its seeds and pods. There are several types of laburnum, some suitable for warm climate gardens, others for cool, but all are poisonous, which is unfortunate because this is an extremely beautiful tree. However, several hybrids which rarely set seed have been developed, which reduces the risk of poisoning, e.g. *L. watereii* and *L. vossi*. Laburnums reach about 7 metres.

Wisteria (*Wisteria floribunda* and *sinensis*) One of Australia's favourite introduced vines with its gorgeous hanging clusters of blue-mauve flowers in spring. Widely grown to shade verandahs, patios and arbours or to cover unsightly sheds

Even the seeds of the lovely wisteria are poisonous

and garages. Unfortunately, the pods and seeds have caused poisoning in children in many countries, producing mild to severe gastro-enteritis with repeated vomiting, abdominal pain and diarrhoea and sometimes collapse. No deaths have been reported.

Oleander (*Nerium oleander*) Originally from the Mediterranean area, this beautiful flowering shrub grows in great clumps almost everywhere in Australia, a favourite because its pink, white and rose coloured flowers put on a spectacular show for literally months of the year. Considering this, and considering that all parts of the plant are extremely toxic, it is surprising that poisoning in children is quite rare. Most human poisoning has been due to eating the flowers, chewing twigs or eating food cooked or stirred with oleander stems. Even the smoke

The poisonous oleander grows almost everywhere in Australia

from oleander cuttings deposited on barbecue food can make children sick. The newly-opened flowers are particularly poisonous; children have died after eating just one or two. A bushy, leathery-leaved shrub to 3 metres.

Privet (*Ligustrum vulgare*) The days of the privet hedge may be numbered as many people believe it should be declared a noxious weed … which would be a good thing as many cases of poisoning in children have been reported overseas, in Sydney and in Melbourne. It is uncertain at this stage whether it is the berries or the leaves of the privet which are the culprit. Symptoms are severe gastric irritation, pain, vomiting, purging, drowsiness and difficulty in movement. There is also some evidence that the inconspicuous but strong-smelling white flowers contribute to asthmatic attacks. All in all, the privet is *not* the best plant for the home garden. Unclipped, the privet will grow to a large shrub over 3 metres tall.

Daphne (*Daphne odora*) It is hard to believe this beautifully perfumed small shrub with its lovely clusters of pink and white shaded flowers and neat woody habit is poisonous. Yet that is true. There are numerous cases in overseas literature of poisoning in women and children who have eaten the succulent fruits or chewed the bark of this favourite ornamental … only a few berries are needed to kill a child. Fortunately, daphne berries are uncommon, most plants failing to set seed. Daphne grows to about 1 metre.

Blue Flax Lily (*Dianella*) This pretty perennial familiar to those who cultivate rock gardens is on the suspects list. Not much is known about its toxicity, but it seems the fruits are poisonous. A child died in New Zealand after eating the fruits of this plant and an experienced bushman, after eating one fruit only, was overcome with an overwhelming desire to swing to the left when walking.

Broad Bean (*Vicia faba*) To most people, to almost everyone in fact, the Broad Bean is a delicious spring vegetable to be enjoyed without worry. To certain people of Mediterranean origin — and generally these people know that they are at risk because they have a long family medical history — eating the seeds or inhaling the pollen of the cultivated broad bean can produce acute toxic anaemia.

Puncture Wounds in the Garden

Deep puncture wounds, such as those resulting from stepping on sharp rusty nails, should always be treated as potentially dangerous. Any germs which have entered the wound will not as easily be washed away by blood flow as from an open cut, and unless the child's tetanus boosters are up to date, a visit to the doctor should be made.

Mowing Safely

Make sure children are not playing on the lawn while you are mowing. Eye and other injuries can result from flying stones or other hard objects hit by the mower blades.

More Poisonous Plants

Monkshood (*Aconitum napellus*) All parts are toxic if eaten

Apple of Sodom (*Solanum sodomaeum*) The fruit is poisonous to humans

Black nightshade (*Solanum nigrum*) The green berries of this common weed are poisonous

Cardinal flower (*Lobelia cardinalis*) All parts are poisonous

Crepe jasmine (*Ervatamia coronaria*) All parts are toxic to humans

Cunjevoi (*Alocasia macrorrhiza*) Fatal poisonings reported in children who ate flowers, leaves or stems

Deadly nightshade (*Atropa belladonna*) Only a few berries can kill a small child

Dumbcane (*Dieffenbachia* spp). Only a few berries of this popular indoor plant can poison a young child and cause death

Golden dewdrop (*Duranta repens*) The berries are poisonous

Glory lily (*Gloriosa superba*) All parts of this plant are poisonous, especially the root

Lily of the Valley (*Convallaria majalis*) All parts are poisonous if eaten

Madeira winter cherry (*Solanum pseudocapsicum*) The berries of this plant are poisonous

Pencil bush (*Euphorbia tirucalli*) Not only is the sap of this popular indoor plant highly poisonous if eaten, but if it gets in the eye it causes temporary blindness

Poinsettia (*Euphorbia pulcherrima*) The sap of this plant is poisonous and a skin irritant

Poison Ivy (*Toxicodendron radicans*) Sap, leaves and fruit are poisonous to eat and the plant can irritate skin on contact

Rhubarb (*Rheum rhaponticum*) The leaf blade of the rhubarb is poisonous to eat

Toadstools (*Amanita* spp.) Better to accidentally destroy a few mushrooms than risk eating a toadstool, which can result in anything from hallucinations to death

Wintersweet (*Acokanthera spectabilis*) The fruit especially, but also other parts of the plant, are toxic to eat and also cause skin irritation

Cerberus (*Cerbera manghas*) Seeds and milky sap poisonous

Philodendron (*Philodendron* spp.) This very commonly grown indoor plant can cause intoxication in young children, though no deaths have been reported

Apple (*Malus* spp.) Leaves or seeds in large amounts are toxic

Apricot (*Prunus armeniaca*) Kernels in large amounts are toxic

Almond (*Prunus dulcis*) The kernels of the bitter type are toxic

Hemlock (*Conium maculatum*) If large amounts are eaten, it is poisonous

Lantana (*Lantana camara*) The green fruits of this common plant are poisonous

Potatoes (*Solanum tuberosum*) The green skin of potatoes exposed to light is said to cause vomiting, abdominal pain and diarrhoea

Native loquat (*Rhodomyrtus macrocarpa*) Fruits cause blindness

Everyday Plants that Irritate Skin or Eyes

Scarlet Rhus (*Toxicodendron succedaneum*) The botanical name of this commonly cultivated tree means Poison Tree — which seems to say all that is necessary. Severe skin irritation has been noted on the legs, face and arms of many children who have climbed rhus trees, and even adults who are sensitive will swell up in the face and hands after picking or pruning it. Often called Japanese Wax Tree, or Sumach, the Rhus is a spectacular, totally hairless, sparsely branched tree, colouring to a incredibly rich red in autumn, and dramatised by huge hanging clusters of cherry-sized fruit which are used for wax by the Japanese, and which remain after leaf-fall, giving the tree a dramatic winter appearance. *Rhus* grows well in all temperate climates. To 11 metres.

Norfolk Island Hibiscus (*Lagunaria patersonia*) This handsome pyramidal tree with its distinctive leathery leaves, grey-green on top and mealy white underneath, and its masses of single rose-pink flowers, seems made to flourish in the salt-laden winds of coastal gardens, yet it is not an advisable plant for a garden where children will play. Known as the Cow Itch or Sore Eye Tree, its hard, walnut-sized, inedible fruits have tiny invisible barbed hairs on them which are extremely irritating to both humans and animals. A fast grower, easily propagated from seed, it will grow to 16 metres.

Sticky Weed (*Parietaria judaica*) This unpleasant weed that grows to about half a metre in height causes an extremely itchy raised red rash wherever it has touched the skin of those people unfortunate enough to be susceptible to it. The rash will persist for days. Unfortunately, as this plant flowers so profusely, its incidence is spreading. Best to use gloves when pulling it out, and then wash carefully all exposed skin immediately afterwards.

Other plants reported as being allergy-inducing include:

Most Euphorbias: this includes the poinsettia (*Euphorbia pulcherrima*) and the Rubber Bush or Naked Lady (*Euphorbia tirucalli*). It is the milky sap of these plants that is the trouble-maker: if the sap gets in the eye, it can cause temporary blindness.

Davidson's Plum or Queensland Itch Tree (*Davidsonia pruriensis*) Another tree whose fruits have tiny hairs which irritate skin and eyes.

Other Culprits: Chrysanthemums. Primula. Robyn Gordon Grevillea. Rose thorns. Pollen of grasses such as couch, wild oats and capeweed.

Keep the Garden Tidy

The best way to avoid childhood accidents in the backyard is simply to practise good housekeeping. Make sure all pesticides, weedicides, mower fuels and pool chemicals are stored carefully out of reach. Make sure railings round verandahs are safe and covers over fishponds secure (chicken wire is not necessarily good enough in both these cases). Make sure rakes are left with the tines turned downwards. Check regularly for funnel-web spider holes and clear out rubbish regularly so it cannot harbour undesirables like snakes and spiders. Mow the clover in the grass frequently so bare summer feet won't get bee stings. Make sure shaky or rotting tree limbs are sawn off. Replace worn swing ropes. Always close gates to road or pool and make sure safety gates are kept well maintained. Keep the approaches to flights of outdoor steps clear to minimise tripping.

Thorny trees and shrubs are unsuitable for gardens where children play. Berberis. Large cacti and other succulents with spines. Coral trees. Gleditschia. Hawthorn. The Silk Floss Tree (*Chorisa speciosa*). All these are plants to be avoided if you are likely to have children playing in the garden.

Avoid planting spikes

11 I Wish ... Fantasy Time

If you were a millionaire, what fun it would be to plant a garden for your children incorporating all the exotic delights from garden history plus a few others that modern technology has made possible. A sampling of the things you might choose is wistfully included below.

A maze. The maze has a long historic pedigree starting back in the days when the English garden was a park, large house parties lasted weeks and gardeners were sufficiently plentiful to keep the head-high hedges of the labyrinth clipped to perfection. Mazes were devised not only as a pleasant adult game but also as a garden ornament: many of the early mazes were low, so they were therefore to be surveyed as well as walked in, and incorporated sweet smelling herbs and coloured flowers. Children, however, love the high mazes in which you are invited to get lost ... but Australian children are especially underprivileged in this department. The only living green maze that I know of in Australia is situated in the grounds of the Military College at Duntroon in the suburbs of Canberra. It is an excellent example of the genre, well-maintained and formed from clipped cotoneaster hedges. If you are in Canberra and want to treat the children, ask the officer of the day there if it is OK to see it. The day they let me in the maze was given extra piquancy by the fact that one of those big sprinklers that pump themselves round in a circle was playing on one corner. We not only had to negotiate that corner without getting lost, but negotiate it with the sprinkler coming closer, closer, closer. Amid shrieks, we got thoroughly doused not only once, but twice, which attests to the difficulty of the maze...

An outdoor theatre. Nothing is more charming than a performance outdoors on a beautiful summer evening. The Greeks knew it. The Romans knew it. So do the opera buffs at Glyndebourne. Just imagine the concerts your children would put on on a raised-step grass stage, with cypress hedges for wings and a backdrop of thick clipped cypress, while you recline admiringly on a deck chair under the stars. See colour plate page 84.

Topiary — the most fantastic garden art. Rich men in every country of the world throughout history have decorated their gardens with this most artificial and most light-hearted of garden arts. If you were a millionaire, imagine the fun of

93

Feeding the elephant in the topiary garden

developing your own topiary garden. An ark with a troop of green animals perhaps. Or, like a famous European garden, you could recreate an Egyptian landscape with sphinxes and pyramid topiary. There is a topiary garden in England of giant chessmen that survived the last war only because an old retainer on the estate kept it clipped regularly and lovingly for the duration. There is another in Holland where aspects of the topiary garden can be appreciated only from viewpoints high in the castle it surrounds: the chest-high topiary letters to one side of the castle can only be seen this way. The possibilities are endless, limited only by your imagination. A green topiary Stonehenge perhaps? Or the Three Sisters of Katoomba? Ayers Rock?

Ornamental lake. Imagine a lake planted with *Victoria amazonica*, the Royal Water Lily, with its stupendous leaves just waiting to take a child on a fabulous journey to the furthest shore. These are the lily leaves which, when brought

Float across the lake on a huge lily leaf

back from excursions to tropical South America by ninteenth century Englishmen, were such a marvel that they supplied Sir Joseph Paxton with inspiration for his design of the load-bearing structure of the famous Crystal Palace in London. He noted that the strong criss-crossed veins on the under-surface of the leaves gave great buoyancy. The leaves are so large, so buoyant, so platter-like with their 10 cm turned-up rims that a child can easily sit on them and float on the lake like a boat. It may indeed by necessary to be a millionaire to possess and grow these wondrous lilies, however, for being a plant from tropical South America they need a water temperature of 27°C to survive, — you would need to heat the water of your lake during the winter. If you want to make your lake utterly perfect, add an island in the middle and a few inlets traversed by stepping stones.

Every child loves stepping stones

Persian water garden. The ancient Persians built gardens that were invariably described as Paradise; if today you were to build the perfect swimming pool, this would be it: an enclosed Persian water garden, glittering with streams and pools to keep out the heat, splashing fountains, ponds full of golden carp, sunken carpet gardens in a bright tapestry of colours, artificial singing birds in the laden fruit trees, a wonderful dappled shade of green over all, the whole forming a perfect symmetrical pattern of colour as beautiful as a Persian carpet.

Fog garden. The eerie effect of grey mist swirling through a garden at the touch of a button is one of the marvels of modern landscape art. First done by the Japanese and occasionally seen in art galleries or at special festivities, any child whose daddy was a millionaire would love this new technological toy for his eighth birthday.

Model train line. Complex and wondrous tracks that wind for metres round the garden, through miniature tunnels, over overpasses, past cuttings, across elevated railway bridges and operated by a complicated system of signals and points, will be as much a toy of the millionaire himself as of the millionaire's children. The rolling stock of these garden trainlines are often perfect replicas of famous old engines, complete down to the correct colours for British Railways or the Indian Pacific line.

A model railway track in the garden can plunge into tunnels, cross bridges, pull into stations, change lines

Joke fountains. The fun of joke fountains seems to have originated in the Middle Ages. Unwary passers-by are suddenly and unexpectedly wetted by a variety of cleverly devised and hidden pipes, often activated by a hidden switch or spring-loaded step. The variety and ingenuity can be amazing. There are the 'rude' ones: the statue of a lady whose nipples squirt you in the eye when you step up a step to see her better, or the little 'Infant holding his Instrument in both his hands' which squirts cold water when the viewer approaches. Others are simply very wet: the stone dining table and benches which squirt water up under the seat when you sit down, artificial trees that rain water down from their leaves as you sit under them, flights of steps weighted to send jets of water at you as you ascend, even a joke tap that squirts the joker himself by directing a jet of water at the stomach. More benign water fountains have birds that warble as the water passes through their stone beaks, fountains which balance balls on their jets, or rows of fountains where one can walk through unspotted.

You don't have to be a millionaire to provide beauty in the garden. Children find it everywhere.
- Rainbows in the sprinkler
- Spider webs in the early morning dew
- A smooth acorn
- A water drop on a nasturtium leaf rolling like silver mercury
- A transparent cicada's wing — or a Black Prince
- A bird's nest with two eggs in it
- A small ant pulling an enormous crumb
- Fluffy white clouds
- A leaf skeleton

Index

In general, plants are indexed under popular names unless plant is better known by its botanical name. Bold numbers indicate colour plates.